SAP® SOA Integration— Enterprise Service Monitoring

Michał Krawczyk

Michał Krawczyk
SAP® SOA Integration Enterprise Service Monitoring

ISBN: 978-1-5003-3845-9

Editor: Alice Adams

Cover Design: Philip Esch, Martin Munzel

Cover Photo: iStockphoto: #19307003 © svariophoto

Interior Design: Johann-Christian Hanke

All rights reserved.

1st Edition 2014, Gleichen

© 2014 by Espresso Tutorials GmbH

URL: *www.espresso-tutorials.com*

Feedback
We greatly appreciate any kind of feedback you have concerning this book. Please mail us at *info@espresso-tutorials.com*.

I would like to thank my family—
especially my wise and beautiful wife
Ewa for encouraging me to fulfill my
dreams, my parents who stayed up
late helping me figure out every life
decision, and my grandparents
whose hunger for life and knowledge
will always inspire me.

Table of Contents

Foreword

by Marcus Gille,
Global Product Owner
SAP Application Interface Framework

Monitoring and error handling of interfaces is something that every company has to deal with. For one, there are legal reasons: you should, say, have your finance errors resolved to be ready for year-end closing. Second, there are business reasons: customers certainly don't want to wait forever for their orders to be delivered!

Depending on data volume, number of interfaces and error rate, monitoring and error handling of interfaces can be a huge effort, as well as cause significant time delays. It is sometimes the case that multiple people need to be involved in the process: a more technically oriented user resolving errors, and a more functionally oriented user giving business input for corrections.

That's why it is crucial to identify the right tool to make the monitoring and error handling as efficient and effective as possible. With some error handling tools in SOA-based integration scenarios, users even need to deal directly with XML structures. This can be quite technical, so user friendliness is key.

I would like to thank Michal for writing this book and for giving us insights into monitoring tools within SAP application systems for SOA-based services. This book provides a great overview on how to setup error-handling tools and make you more productive in using them. Enjoy the read!

Preface

SAP systems are often linked to multiple systems and applications like external warehouse management systems, external planning applications, or other business partners by using different integration technologies. More and more companies are choosing a SOA paradigm which means, among a few other things, that the interfaces are designed and developed using web service related technologies. Most of those SOA integration scenarios require constant monitoring, both from the business point of view and a technical point of view. On the business front, it's possible that the data in the messages used in the integration may not be correct and may fail in the receiver system due to those errors. From a technical point of view when connectivity is not working, the message may not even reach the receiver system. For companies where SAP is the central system, most of the monitoring and integration scenario error handling happens in a SAP backend system like ECC, SRM, SCM, etc. and that's why SAP provides a range of interface monitoring tools. Those tools include simple monitors, which provide basic functionality (like Local Integration Engine monitor). In addition, they provide more advanced tools, which allow for more sophisticated monitoring and error handling like Forward Error Handling/Error and Conflict Handler to tools, which were built especially to support the build and monitoring phases of any SOA integration scenario in complex integration landscapes like SAP Application Interface Framework.

The content of this book was intended for business users and key users who need to monitor SOA integration scenarios on regular basis and need to understand the basic customizing options for SAP interface monitoring tools, as well as for decision makers who are responsible for determining the correct monitoring tool for their landscape.

This book explains the main differences between the tools in SAP's range of SOA products and readers can expect to get familiarity with the primary functions. This book also provides detailed descriptions of most of the customizing options for Local Integration Engine Monitor, Forward Error Handling/Error and Conflict Hander, and SAP Application Interface Framework so it can serve as a tutorial and most of the examples shown in the book can be immediately implemented in your SAP systems.

We have added a few icons to highlight important information. These include:

Tips

Tips highlight information concerning more details about the subject being described and/or additional background information.

Warnings

Warnings draw attention to information that you should be aware of when you go through the examples from this book on your own.

Finally, a note concerning the copyright: All screenshots printed in this book are the copyright of SAP AG. All rights are reserved by SAP AG. Copyright pertains to all SAP images in this publication. For simplification, we will not mention this specifically underneath every screen-shot.

1 What is SOA integration monitoring and error handling?

What is SOA integration and which kinds of SOA scenarios can we (and in most cases need to) monitor within our SAP landscape so that the business scenarios based on them can run smoothly? We will review the tools available in SAP backend application systems for monitoring SOA scenarios to better understand their advantages and disadvantages.

1.1 SOA Integration

Service oriented architecture (SOA) is a pattern based on a few conditions:

- ▶ All of the services (functions) exposed to the outside world are published in a **platform independent** manner.

- ▶ Services need to be **stable.**

- ▶ Services need to be based on a **commonly known set of fields.**

What does it mean for the SAP? First, it means that different business functions, or parts of business processes, are exposed in the form of web services that can be consumed by other applications. For example, creating a sales order, confirming an outbound delivery, or deleting a customer master record.

Definition of web service

 A web service is a method of communication over the Internet in which the provider of the service allows the consumer to connect to a specific IP address in order to execute a specific function on the provider's system. SAP application systems like ECC, CRM, and SRM primarily use SOAP-based web services. SOAP (Simple Object Access Protocol) is a special protocol for exchanging information over the web services, in most cases based on HTTP (but can also reply on other application protocols), where the message's structure is divided into 4 parts: envelope, header, body, and fault.

As the web service standard is platform independent, then this important requirement is met. When SAP releases changes to any of the published interfaces, those new functions will be exposed as new interfaces (or new versions of the old ones) in order not to change the old versions which needs to work in a stable manner. One of the biggest changes for SAP in terms of SOA compliance was to start using a common set of fields used by other applications as well. In the past, most SAP applications were using IDOC structures to communicate with other applications. However, IDOC structures were designed at SAP to use with other SAP applications, so it was very difficult for non-SAP applications to understand the fields of the IDOC's message structures. To meet the requirement of a commonly used set of fields, all SAP delivered SOA services are based on Global Data Types. These data types are based on international standards (like CCTS).

SAP Global Data Types

 Well documented building blocks for all business objects are based on ISO 15000-5 and UN/CEFACT CCTS standards. They are defined in the Enterprise Service Repository (ESR) of SAP Process Integration and described by XML schemas. Global Data Types are based on Core Data Types (called primary data types which do not have any business semantics).

Using Global Data Types (GDTs) ensures harmonization of the message structures used in different services and the understanding of those structures by other non-SAP applications as well.

SAP Enterprise Services

 When a web service is implemented according to the SOA principles in an SAP backend system it is called an Enterprise Service.

1.2   SOA monitoring and error handling

When services are exposed by SAP application systems other systems can call them and in an ideal world, everything would always work. In reality, many of the calls from the consumer application do not execute properly on the web service provider systems. There can be many reasons for this:

- The consumer sent the **wrong information** (i.e. the message does not contain all of the required fields).

- The consumer sent the message in the **wrong order** (i.e. deletion of a business transaction before creation).

- The consumer sent **incomplete information** (connectivity issues).

- The provider may **not** be **ready** to receive the message (i.e. master data is not synchronized).

- The provider may **not** be **able** to process the information (i.e. the system is down at the moment).

There are many situations in which SOA integration scenarios will not work as planned and need to be fixed immediately. In order to be prepared to handle these cases quickly, some SOA integration scenarios need to be monitored. For some, we need to design and implement a set of proper error handling techniques.

What are the different kinds of SOA integration scenarios? We can divide SOA scenarios into a few categories and decide which of them need to be monitored. The most basic criteria is the difference between synchronous and asynchronous SOA scenarios. Synchronous scenarios always give the resulting information back to the consumer application so in this case, it's not necessary to be able to monitor them on the provider application systems as the consumer will always be aware of the status of the message and can always restart the message. Synchronous applications in most cases also need to be processed very quickly as the other application is waiting for the result. This is the second reason why we don't want to slow them down by doing additional persistence steps in order to be able to monitor them. On the other hand, asynchronous messages cannot be restarted from the consumer application if there is an error because the consumer does not know the status of the message. In this case, the processing speed is also not as important as in the case of synchronous applications. This provides the opportunity to implement a set of monitoring and error handling functions.

The second question is: Where should you monitor SOA integration scenarios? You can do that in a few different types of systems:

▶ **Backend application systems**—this is where the service is implemented and where you can get the most information about it in the event of an error. This is also the system in which the people who are responsible for business transactions have access to as they are constantly working on it.

▶ **Enterprise service bus (ESB)**—many companies utilize a single system that is responsible for connecting all application systems with each other. This is also a good place to monitor interfaces as it is the central point for all SOA mediated scenarios. SAP Process Orchestration is a typical example of an ESB used for such purposes.

▶ **Other monitor applications**—companies can have a rule to send all kinds of errors to a special system used only for error monitoring. In many cases, this is closely coupled with a ticketing system, which can be used for assigning people to different kinds of incidents. SAP Solution Manager is a typical example of system used for this purpose.

17

Mediated SOA integration scenarios vs. point-to-point

 Mediated SOA integration scenarios are designed in such a way that they always use an ESB (Enterprise Service Bus) as a connectivity option between each of the two application systems. Point-to-point scenarios are a direct application to application connections which don't use any other system to communicate with each other.

In this book, we will only concentrate on monitoring and error handling of asynchronous SOA integration scenarios on the backend applications systems like ECC, SCM, etc. for two reasons:

1. Monitoring and error handling of SOA integration scenarios can be initiated in many other places (ESB, external monitoring applications, etc.). However, in most cases in order to be able to find out the real cause of the issue, we need to do the monitoring in the backend application system because this is the place from where we can obtain the most detailed error information and reprocess the transaction.

2. Different companies use different ESBs and external monitoring applications.

Error handling is part of a SOA integration scenario monitoring and is the second most important aspect as the web service layer does not provide any special tools for completing this task. SAP backend application systems can use a wide range of special applications designed for error handling and in Chapter 1.3 we will briefly review them. First, however, we need to define what kind of functions we would expect from these tools:

▶ **Displaying messages** in a readable way for most humans—this means that the message should be easy to read for anyone (not just for people with IT skills).

▶ **Changing the data** of the message—in some cases a message's data (values for certain fields) needs to be changed before reprocessing it.

▶ **Restarting failed messages**—both automated and scheduled.

▶ **Restarting** a specific type of an error—not all errors can be handled in the same way, so it does not make sense to reprocess all messages in the same manner.

▶ **Ability to retrieve the error information**—in an easy way to be able to track down the issue.

▶ **Cancelling the message**—sometimes messages need to be cancelled as the new messages will be distributed from the sender system.

▶ **Error notification**—automated error propagation to the responsible users.

▶ **Linking of messages to transaction/object**—monitoring transactions need to be able to redirect to customizing or transaction data.

▶ **Content-based error searching**—users need to be able to find a message on the basis of specific information stored inside the message.

▶ **Data access authorization**—not all users are allowed to access the content of all messages so there needs to be an authorization framework utilization.

1.3 Tools for monitoring SOA scenarios

A few of the most commonly used applications for monitoring SOA integration scenarios in SAP backend application systems include:

1. **Local Integration Engine monitor**—standard monitor available and enabled in all SAP systems.
2. **Forward Error Handling/Error and Conflict Handler** (FEH/ECH)—additional monitor available in all SAP systems, but not enabled in standard.
3. **SAP Application Integration Framework (AIF)**—additional monitoring component which can be acquired in order to monitor SOA integration scenarios.

1.3.1 Local Integration Engine Monitor

Local Integration Engine Monitor is a standard tool which allows monitoring of SOA scenarios. In order to open the Local Integration Engine Monitor start the transaction code SXMB_MONI and select MONITOR FOR PROCESSED XML MESSAGES, or directly with transaction code SXI_MONITOR.

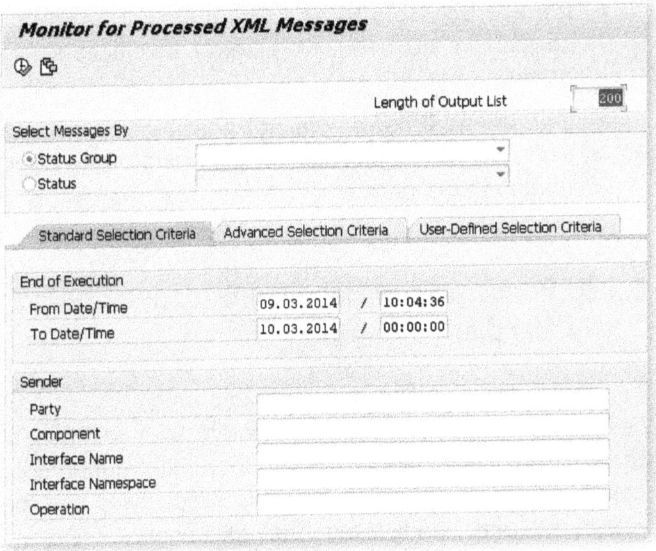

Figure 1.1: Local Integration Engine Monitor

The local Integration Engine Monitor is a very simple tool and some of its functions are available in a limited scope including (see Figure 1.1):

▶ **Payload editor**—payload editor is based on XML message structures so it's very difficult to read for users who are not familiar with XML messages.

▶ **Authorization concept**—it's not possible to restrict access to certain messages on the basis of the content of SOA messages, you can only do that on using message header fields like interface name, sender/receiver system, etc.

▶ **Automated restarting**—it's not possible to restart certain types of errors because restarting is only possible on a more general level.

▶ **Successful message monitoring**—complicated monitoring of successful log messages (i.e. created document numbers for transaction data).

▶ **It's not possible to add tips/hints** for error processing in the event of an error that occurs frequently.

▶ **Document linking**—it's not possible to navigate from the XML message to any customizing table related to the error.

1.3.2 Forward Error Handling/Error and Conflict Handler

Forward Error Handling is a concept which allows processing errors in the provider system with the use of Error and Conflict Handler. Errors that occur during data conversion and business function processing can be monitored and handled by business users or system administrators. You can start this monitor with transaction code ECH_MONI_SEL which will start the Error and Conflict Handler as shown in Figure 1.2.

Error and Conflict Handler is a much more advanced tool compared to the Local Integration Engine monitor. However, there are still some functions that are not available including:

▶ **Outbound asynchronous message monitor**—it's not possible to monitor errors for outbound SOA integration scenarios.

▶ **Successful message monitoring**—Error and Conflict Handler can only monitor messages which resulted in an error—all correctly processed messages still need to be monitored using Local Integration Engine monitor.

▶ **Authorization concept**—it's not possible to restrict access to certain messages on the basis of the content of SOA messages, you can only do that using message header fields like interface name, sender/receiver system, etc.

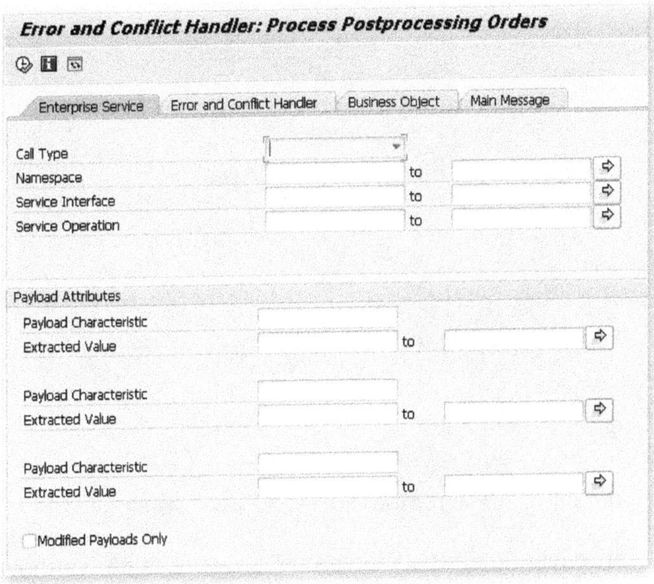

Figure 1.2: ECH monitor

1.3.3   SAP Application Interface Framework

SAP Application Interface Framework is an add-on for SAP Business Suite systems which, among many other functions, has a business user friendly user interface implementation and provides a set of very sophisticated SOA monitoring and error handling tools.

23

You can start this monitor shown in Figure 1.3 with transaction code /AIF/ERR.

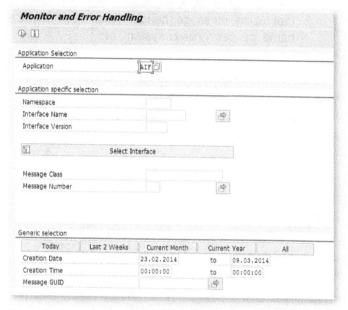

Figure 1.3: AIF error monitor—SAP GUI version

Application Interface Framework appears to be the most powerful of the three tools mentioned as it has all the missing functionality of the previous tools, but it also has a few drawbacks:

▶ **Automated restarting**—available as of AIF 2.0 service pack 03 only.

▶ **License cost**—as it's a separate add-on from SAP, it requires an additional license.

In the following chapters, we will explore how to customize those three tools in order to be able to maximize their full potential.

2 Local Integration Engine Monitor

Local Integration Engine Monitor is the most well known and most commonly used application for monitoring SOA integration scenarios in backend application systems. There's very little configuration required to make it run, but it has some features which can make it much easier to use. We will explore those features in this chapter.

2.1 Activation and initial configuration

In standard SAP, the Local Integration Engine Monitor does not require any activation and both kinds of asynchronous web services (mediated and point-to-point) will run through this monitor.

2.2 Message monitoring and error monitoring

Message monitoring and error monitoring is done with the same tool—transaction SXMB_MONI • MONITOR FOR PROCESSES XML MESSAGES, or directly from transaction SXI_MONITOR.

There are a number of standard selection criteria like sender/receiver interface name, namespace, system, as well as some more advanced selection criteria like Message ID, Error ID, etc. (see Figure 2.1).

Monitor for Processed XML Messages

⊕ ⓑ

Length of Output List [200]

Select Messages By
- ● Status Group [▼]
- ○ Status [▼]

| Standard Selection Criteria | Advanced Selection Criteria | User-Defined Selection Criteria |

Message ID [ ] ⇨

Message Type [ ]
From Date/Time Sent [ ] / 00:00:00
To Date/Time Sent [ ] / 00:00:00
From Execution Start Date/Time [ ] / 00:00:00
To Execution Start Date/Time [ ] / 00:00:00
Logical Pipeline ID [ ]
Error ID [ ]   Error Category [ ]
Status Details [ ]
Client [ ]   User [ ]
Technical Inbound Channel [ ]   Technical Outbound C [ ]
Outbound Status [▼]
Queue ID [ ]
With Acknowledgment Messages ☐

Figure 2.1: Advanced selection criteria

After we run the selection, we can see all of the messages. If we double-click on any of them, we can see the contents of the message in the INBOUND MESSAGE • PAYLOADS • MAIN DOCUMENT section (see Figure 2.2).

Display XML Message Versions

&Window 1 &Window 2 🗔Window 1 🗔Window 2 🗔 🗐 ⊕Restart ✎ 🗐 🗚Error Information

▾ ⬜ XML Message   Msg ID = 1FF315E0AAC41
  ▾ ◪ Inbound Message (RECEIVER)
    ▸ ⬜ SOAP Header
    ▸ ⬜ SOAP Body
    ▾ ⬜ Payloads
      • ▣ MainDocument (application/xml)

– <MessageHeader>
    <CreationDateTime>**0002-11-**
      30T00:00:00Z</CreationDateTime>
  </MessageHeader>
– <PurchaseOrder reconciliationPeriodCounterValue="**0**"
    itemListCompleteTransmissionIndicator="**true**">

Figure 2.2: Content of the SOAP message

In the event of an error, we will be able to see the red flag and short status on the first screen of the application.

If the web service was using a fault message type and was programmed correctly, then we can see some additional details by clicking on the red flag as shown in Figure 2.3 below.

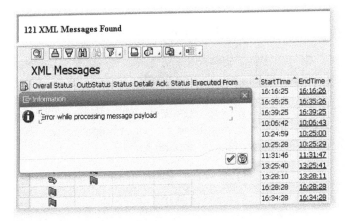

Figure 2.3: Error monitoring

Fault message type

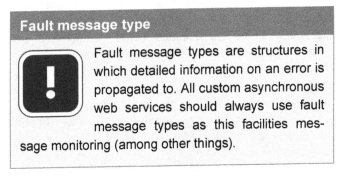

Fault message types are structures in which detailed information on an error is propagated to. All custom asynchronous web services should always use fault message types as this facilities message monitoring (among other things).

A more detailed error description, or any other error information, can always be found by drilling down into the message content (double-click on the message) and by opening the error section of the SOAP HEADER as shown in Figure 2.4.

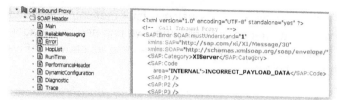

Figure 2.4: Error section of the SOAP header

As we can see, message and error monitoring with the use of Local Integration Engine Monitor is primarily done with the use of XML messages. The expectation is that the user knows how to work with XML standard. For that reason, it is not very user friendly compared to other SAP SOA integration monitoring tools.

2.3 Message reprocessing

Message reprocessing is one of the most typical tasks during day-to-day work with SOA integration scenarios. Messages tend to fail for different reasons and they either need to be reprocessed (which in some cases means that the content of the message also needs to be changed), or cancelled. A message which cannot or should not be reprocessed needs to be cancelled. A cancelled message is the only identification that an error was checked and proper action was taken. You can cancel messages directly from monitoring transaction by selecting the message that you want to cancel and EDIT • CANCEL MESSAGE WITH ERRORS from the menu (see Figure 2.5).

It's also possible to cancel messages from a special program called RSXMB_CANCEL_MESSAGES. In the event that you need to cancel a lot of messages, it is advisable to run it with this program.

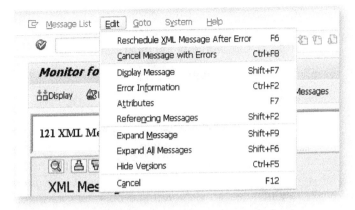

Figure 2.5: Cancelling messages from the message monitor

RSXMB_CANCEL_MESSAGES—test mode

Each time you use this special program to cancel messages, you should run it first in the test mode to see if the selection criteria you've used selects the correct messages. Only after you're sure that the selection was correct, run the program once more without test mode turned on.

If we know that the message can be reprocessed manually, which means that the error should no longer happen, we can deal with it similarly as cancelling the message. We need to select the message and click on the RESTART button in the menu (see Figure 2.6).

Figure 2.6: Restarting messages from transaction SXMB_MONI

However, unlike message cancelling manual restarting does not occur very often. Messages can fail due to number of reasons, some of the most common are:

▶ missing master data

▶ locked objects

In those cases, sometimes we don't need any manual intervention so we can schedule automated message reprocessing with the program RSXMB_RESTART_ MESSAGES. In typical landscapes, we run this program every few minutes so that interface operators can concentrate on the issues which cannot be reprocessed automatically and, in most cases, require some other manual intervention.

2.4   Content-based Message Search

One of the most typical tasks while performing SOA integration scenarios monitoring is searching for messages. You either need to find a few incorrect messages among many other failed messages if there are only a few that you need to take care of in the first place, or someone from the business team may not be sure if one of the messages got processed and needs to search among the successfully processed messages to confirm that integration scenario was executed correctly at the messaging layer too. In such cases, a typical search criteria like:

▶ sender system

▶ interface name

▶ interface namespace, etc.

may not be enough as we want to do a search on the basis of the content of the message with the use of some significant fields which are unique for a single message, like order number, delivery number, material number, etc. In order to do that with the Local Integration Engine monitor, we need to customize the monitor using transaction SXMS_LMS_CONF. There are two things that need to be customized:

▶ **Filter**—this is where you determine which mes- sage type you'd like to search for content-based message values.

▶ **Search Criteria**—configuration that specifies which values of the payload will be used for searching.

In order to create a new filter, you need to use the ADD NEW FILTER button (the one with plus icon from Figure 2.7 below).

Figure 2.7: Adding a new filter

On the filter creation screen you need to populate the mandatory values (see Figure 2.8):

▶ Name—provide the interface name.

▶ Namespace—provide the interface namespace.

The rest of the values are not required, but if you want to limit indexing of unnecessary messages you can also populate them.

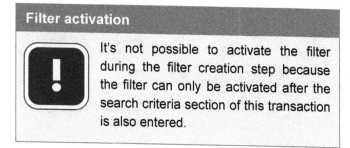

Figure 2.8: Filter creation

Filter activation

It's not possible to activate the filter during the filter creation step because the filter can only be activated after the search criteria section of this transaction is also entered.

Once the filter is created, double-click on the filter and move to the bottom of the screen in order to find the SEARCH CRITERIA section. We can add the new criteria in the same way that we created the filter by using the button with the ADD icon. On the new SEARCH CRITERIA screen enter the name of the search criteria, which in most cases would be similar to the name of the type of value we're looking for. We also need to enter the XPath to the value of field in the message that we want to use for searching. In the example from Figure 2.9, we will be searching for the purchase order number which has a field name ID in the node (XML Segment) Purchase Order.

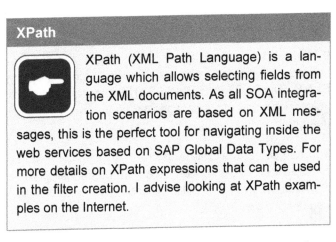

Figure 2.9: Search criteria creation

XPath

XPath (XML Path Language) is a language which allows selecting fields from the XML documents. As all SOA integration scenarios are based on XML messages, this is the perfect tool for navigating inside the web services based on SAP Global Data Types. For more details on XPath expressions that can be used in the filter creation. I advise looking at XPath examples on the Internet.

The second way to define the search criteria apart from using the XPath, is to use a Dynamic Header. This kind of extractor searches for adapter specific message attributes from SAP Process Orchestration.

By default, the content-based message values will be extracted during the processing of new messages (EX-TRACT DURING MESSAGE PROCESSING). However, if you want to search the messages that were already processed you need to select the second option—EXTRACT WITH EXTERNAL JOB.

Once the search criteria is created, you need to go and activate the filter in change mode by selecting the ACTI-VATE checkbox. Once you do that, the status of the Search Criteria will become green as shown in Figure 2.10, which means that the filter is working.

Figure 2.10: Activated Filter

If you need to search for values from the already processed messages we need to run program SXMS_EXTRACT_MESSAGES. This program will index values from the old messages so they can be used for searching.

You can select the criteria in order to minimize the time required to run the indexing program by choosing some filter values. In Figure 2.11 we choose to index all messages from the last 60 minutes only.

Indexing

 Indexing content-based message search means searching for values from a pre-defined set of filters and putting them into a separate table where the can be accessed quickly, without the need to search the content of the whole message again.

User-Defined Indexing

Selection

  Date/Time

    ⊙ Time Interval

      Extract Messages from Last   60 Minute(s)

    ○ Times

      Execute From   21.03.2014 / 17:51:50

      Execute up to   22.03.2014 / 17:51:50

Sender

  Partners

  Schema

  Agency

  Communication Component

  Interface Name

  Interface Namespace

Recipient

  Partners

  Schema

  Agency

  Communication Component

  Interface Name

  Interface Namespace

Figure 2.11: Indexing program for already processed messages

In the program output, you can already see if the extraction was successful. If the search criteria for a customized filter is visible as in Figure 2.12 below and any kind of value is populated, that means the filter is working and can be used for searching messages later on.

Figure 2.12: Extraction log

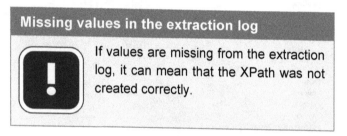

We can test if the filter is working in transaction SXMB_MONI by selecting the USER-DEFINED SELECTION CRITERIA and by populating it with the value of the field which should be used for searching as shown in Figure 2.13 below.

If the selection was successful, then on the result output screen we should be able to see only the message with the specified value in the content. When we select it and use the ATTRIBUTES button from the menu, as shown in Figure 2.14 below, we should be able to see all Search Criteria defined for those messages.

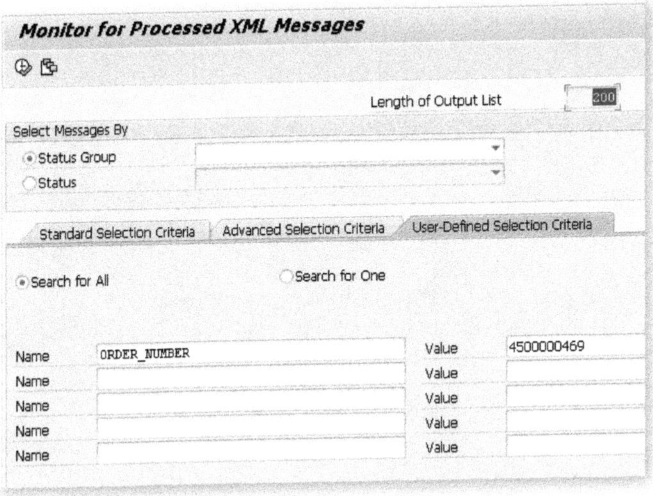

Figure 2.13: User-defined message search in SXMB_MONI

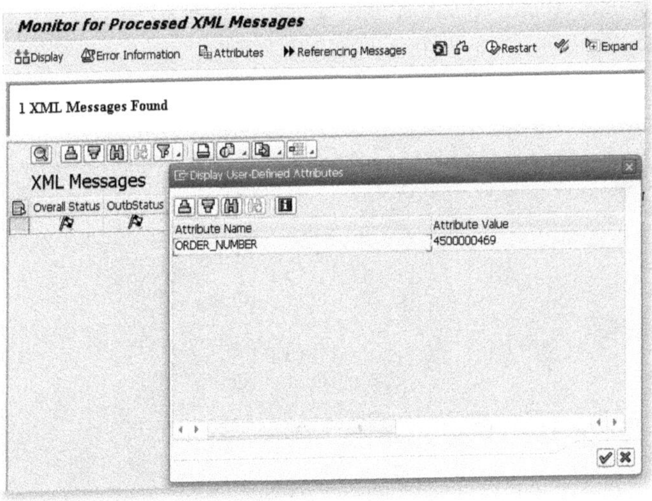

Figure 2.14: Content-based attributes of the message

3 Forward Error Handling and Error and Conflict Handler

Forward Error Handling (FEH) together with Error and Conflict Handler (ECH) are the tools that work together with Local Integration Monitor, but extend many of its limitations. In this chapter, we will take a closer look at the advanced features of both FEH and ECH.

3.1 Concept

Forward Error Handling is a framework designed on systems with an ABAP backend, meaning most SAP application systems (ECC, SRM, CRM, etc.). You can utilize this framework to implement SOA integration scenarios for inbound messages (service providers). The idea behind the concept is that according to SAP development best practices for asynchronous communication (in contrast to synchronous communication), the receiving systems should be responsible for solving the error instead of propagating the error information back to the sender system. The receiving system is closer to the root of the error and in most cases, it will be much easier to solve it there. While it's possible to use acknowledgments to notify the sender, not many applications in the SOA world can work with them. The FEH concept is an alternative approach to the majority of SOA integration scenarios.

What are acknowledgments?

 Acknowledgments are a type of message distributed from the receiver system to the sender system that enable sending confirmation messages that nofity that the receiver application received the message from the sender. SAP distinguishes two types of acknowledgments: system, which are used by the runtime and confirm that the messages were received and application, which confirm the status of the processed message at the receiver application (successfully processed or not). In case using SAP-to-SAP communication for SOA integration scenarios, it's possible to use acknowledgments with ABAP proxies.

Most SAP standard Enterprise Services use the FEH concept and new, custom SOA services should also be developed in a way in which they can work according to the FEH framework. This means that if the application issues an error message, the receiver will not reject the message and will not send any information back to the sender. Instead, the receiver system will try to solve the issue itself either by restarting the message in case of a temporary error, or will notify business users which can help solving it either by correcting the message, changing the customizing settings, or in some cases by entering transactional or master data.

Forward Error Handling in SAP applications is implemented using the Error and Conflict Handler (ECH), which is a tool used for solving errors initiated by asynchronous message processes. Error and Conflict Handler works heavily with two internal components:

- Post Processing Office (PPO)—Responsible for creating and processing orders (all messages processed with PPO are called orders).

- Hierarchical Derivation Service (HDS)—Responsible for determining the correct resolution strategy.

The relationship between FEH and ECH

 The Forward Error Handling concept is implemented in SAP ABAP backend systems with the use of Error and Conflict Handler so both of them work closely together. From the SOA Integration monitoring perspective, we can regard them as the same tool.

3.2 Activation and initial configuration

Most SAP standard Enterprise Services as of enhancement package 5 for ERP 6.0, use FEH/ECH by default. In order to start using it as an additional (to Local Integration Engine Monitor) monitor, we only need to activate it. Activation of FEH/ECH is a global setting that affects all Enterprise Services where FEH/ECH has been implemented. In the case of custom build SOA integration scenarios, there's a set of coding rules that need to be implemented so the scenario can start using the full power of FEH/ECH. As this book is focused on monitoring, we will only concentrate on customizing the monitoring features and less on the interface development related activities.

In order to activate the Forward Error Handling and Error and Conflict Hander, you need to open customizing and using the following menu path create a new table entry as shown in Figure 3.1: SPRO • CROSS-APPLICATION COMPONENTS PROCESSES AND TOOLS FOR ENTERPRISE APPLICATIONS • ENTERPRISE SERVICES ERROR AND CONFLICT HANDLER • ACTIVATE ERROR AND CONFLICT HANDLER.

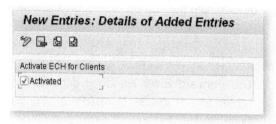

Figure 3.1: FEH/ECH activation

This activity will enable FEH/ECH for all SAP standard Enterprise Services where FEH was used.

3.3   Message monitoring and error monitoring

Message monitoring using FEH/ECH is distributed among two transactions. When the message is processed successfully, we can only monitor it in the Local Integration Engine Monitor with all its limitations. If there was an error in the initial status of the message, only then can the message be monitored in Post Processing Office (PPO) of FEH/ECH.

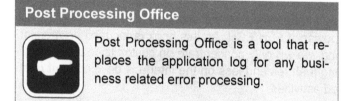

Post Processing Office

Post Processing Office is a tool that replaces the application log for any business related error processing.

You can start the SOA integration scenario monitoring by using transaction SXI_MONITOR, which opens up the Local Integration Engine Monitor. If the message is not successful and FEH/ECH was activated and implemented for the provider service, we can see the new status icon (green arrow) next to the message as shown in Figure 3.2. This specifies that the message was forwarded to the external application, which would be the Post Processing Office.

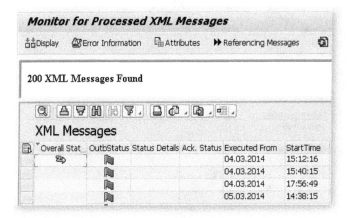

Figure 3.2: Link between Local Integration Engine Monitor and Post Processing Office

---

Local Integration Engine Monitor in FEH/ECH

It's still always possible to display the message in Local Integration Engine Monitor, but there's no need to do that if the service is using FEH/ECH as Post Processing Office is much more advanced monitor compared to the Local Integration Engine Monitor.

If we select the icon for transfer to the external application, we are taken directly to the Post Processing Office. Alternatively, we can use transaction ECH_MONI_SEL, which opens the initial screen of PPO where you can find many selection criteria for searching messages as shown in Figure 3.3.

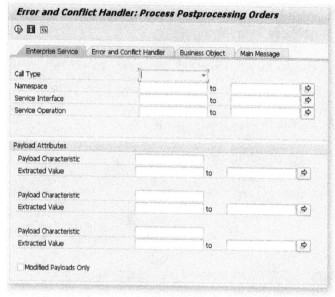

Figure 3.3: Selection criteria from transaction ECH_MONI_SEL

As the selection criteria we can use:

▶ Technical message attributes like service interface, service operation, namespace, etc.

▶ Values from the content of the message—payload attributes.

▶ Business related information—business process and component.

Business Process and Component

Business Process and Component are types of objects linked to messages, used in PPO to segregate messages which resulted in an error.

Once we open up the selection in transaction ECH_MONI_SEL, we should be able to see the error messages segregated by the main object together with the error description in the status column as shown in Figure 3.4.

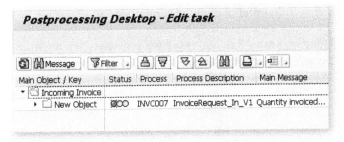

Figure 3.4: Error message on the initial screen of PPO

3.3.1 Post Processing Office detailed screen

If we double-click on the entry, the transaction takes us to the detailed screen of the Post Processing Office. The detailed screen is divided into four areas as shown in Table 3.1.

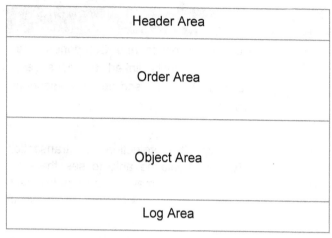

Header Area
Order Area
Object Area
Log Area

Table 3.1: Areas of detailed screen for PPO

Header area—the header area provides the most important information about the error such as the main object used in the message, business process description (which in many cases would be the service interface name of the enterprise service used in SOA integration scenario), main error message which caused the failure, and order status (the status of the message processing). You can also enter a short comment that will be recorded when you save or process the selected entry. A typical header area is shown in Figure 3.5.

Service Interface

 Service interface is an object used to describe a set of operations that will be developed on the service provider system.

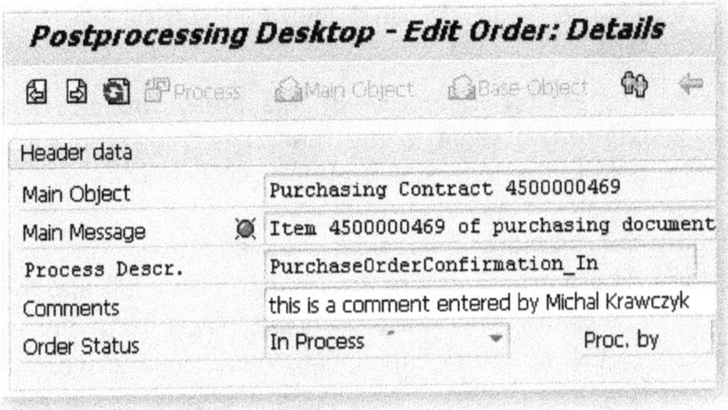

Figure 3.5: Header area of PPO detailed screen

Order area—the order area contains more detailed information on the status of the processed message and consists of several tabs. The main difference between the header area and the order area is that the second one can be fully customized by adding new tabs, changing their order, and hiding some of the tabs. Figure 3.6 shows a set of standard tabs used in the order details screen.

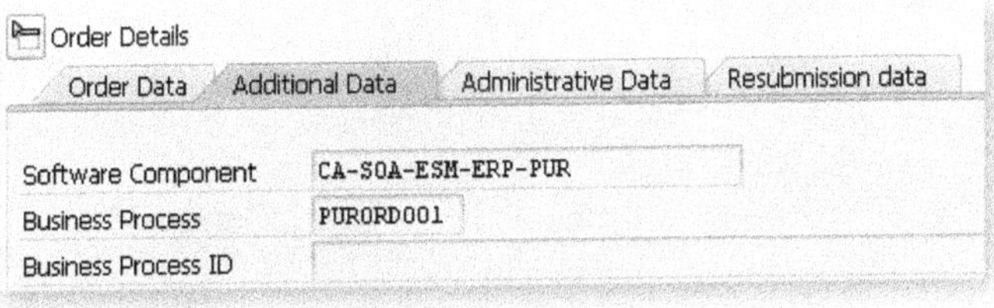

Figure 3.6: Order area of PPO detailed screen

Object area—the objects area provides information, not only about the values used in the message, but can also link them to other objects in the SAP system. As with the order detail area, the object area can also be customized, but in this case on two levels:

47

▶ Tab area—In this area, you can add or hide new tabs.

▶ Processing methods—In this area, you can link different objects to the message fields and navigate to them directly from the PPO screens.

Figure 3.7 displays the object area of one of the messages. There are two tabs: the MESSAGE DATA tab and the PURCHASING CONTRACT tab. The MESSAGE DATA tab is linked to the content of the XML message and we can either display or change its values. We also see a second tab, which for this particular enterprise service is a link to the Purchasing Contract. This means that we can immediately navigate to transactions or master data from the PPO screen which makes it very easy to investigate errors.

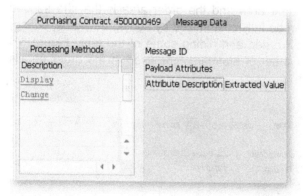

Figure 3.7: Object area of PPO detailed screen

Log area—The log area contains all of the messages generated by the system during processing of the SOA Integration scenario. We can filter out types of messages by clicking on their symbols (STOP, ERROR, WARNING, SUCCESS, etc.) or double-clicking on the message to view more details. If we want to change the size of the window, we can use EXPAND LOG icon to increase the log area to the full screen size. It's also possible to create hints for solving errors which can be linked to the messages in the log and they can also be displayed in the log area. Figure 3.8 shows filtered error messages with hints available in the PPO HINT column.

Figure 3.8: Log area of PPO detailed screen

3.3.2 Payload Editor in Post Processing Ofice

We can open the Payload Editor tool from the Post Processing Office by selecting the DISPLAY processing option from the Message Data tab in the Object area.

Once the Payload Editor is opened, we can see the XML structure of the message in the form of hierarchical format. Data from each node can be displayed by selecting the appropriate table node as shown in Figure 3.9.

Payload Details

	Name of the Data Object	Contents
▼ STRUC_POCONF_POST_MAPPING	Purchasing Document	4500000469
· BAPIMEPOHEADER	Company Code	
· BAPIMEPOHEADERX	Purchasing Doc. Type	
▶ BAPIMEPOITEM	Deletion Indicator	
▶ BAPIMEPOITEMX	Status	
· BAPIMEPOSCHEDULE	Created on	00.00.0000
· BAPIMEPOSCHEDULX	Created by	
· BAPIMECONFHEADER	Item Number Interval	00000
· BAPIMECONFHEADERX	Vendor	
· BAPIMECONF_T_ITEM	Language Key	
· BAPIMECONF_T_ITEMX	ISO code for language key	
▶ BAPIMECONF_T_DETAIL	Terms of Payment	
▶ BAPIMECONF_T_DETAILX		
▶ MESSAGES		

Figure 3.9: Payload editor data view

There are two types of payload:

▶ Pre-mapping payload –This type of payload occurs when the data from the proxy structure cannot be mapped to the data structure of the calling BAPI. A typical case would be a custom service that inserts data into the custom table.

▶ Post-mapping payload—This type of payload occurs when the data from the proxy structure can be mapped to the data structure of the calling BAPI.

BAPI

 A Business Application Programming Interface (BAPI) is a precisely defined interface providing access to methods of objects in an SAP backend application system.

The data display is much more easily used than the XML display in the Local Integration Engine monitor and can be easily used by business people. There's a set of additional functions which can be done in the Payload editor including:

Searching—The SEARCH button is located above the payload details which allows you to search for data in all nodes as per Figure 3.10.

Editing—in some cases it may be necessary to change the message data before reprocessing it because it's not possible to resend the message from the sender system. In this situation, we can use the edit function by clicking on the CHANGE button. It's possible to add new rows, copy rows, and remove rows. It's even possible to use the input help in case the message was mapped to an SAP structure as shown in the Figure 2.11.

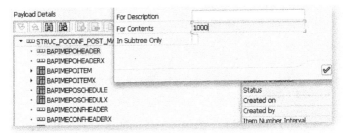

Figure 3.10: Search function in Payload Editor

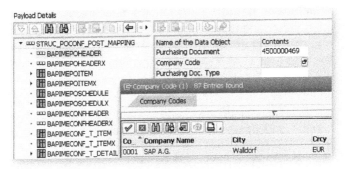

Figure 3.11: Inserting the data in the Payload Editor

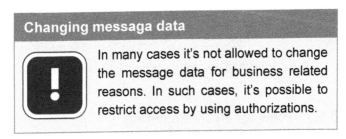

Changing messaga data

In many cases it's not allowed to change the message data for business related reasons. In such cases, it's possible to restrict access by using authorizations.

Versioning—If it's required to make a lot of changes to the data, you can keep track of those changes by creating different versions of the message. In order to use this function, select the SAVE AS NEW VERSION button after making a change as shown in Figure 3.12.

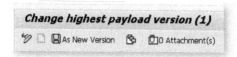

Figure 3.12: Saving a new version of a message in Payload Editor

Keep in mind that the data is not written to the database until you save it with the normal SAVE button.

Attachment handling—When it's necessary to document the changes made to the content of the message, it's possible to upload any kind of file and attach it in the Payload Editor. As it's not very convenient to determine the changes in different structures among different message versions, it's a good practice to add a text document that sums up all changes made to the message content and upload it as an attachment. In order to do that, we need to select the ATTACHMENT button and select the file as shown in Figure 3.13.

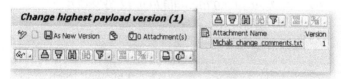

Figure 3.13: Adding attachments in Payload Editor

3.3.3 Hints for error monitoring

Whenever SOA interface monitoring is done with the help of Error and Conflict Handler, we may encounter a number of different types of errors during message processing. Some of them may not happen very often, others may be more frequent, but in all cases it's always a good practice to document how the issue was solved. Error and Conflict Handler provides the opportunity to assign hints to each error type where we can describe how the error was solved. In the log area of the detailed Error and Conflict Handler screen we can find all messages and for each of those we can assign a HINT as shown in Figure 3.14.

Ty.. Message Text
Quantity invoiced greater than goods receipt quantity
LTxt PPO...
Create Hint for Message
Display Hint for Process

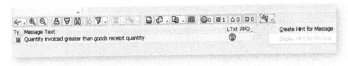

Figure 3.14: Hint creation

Next, we need to populate the hint's information area as shown in Figure 3.15 with the pertinent information that can be used to help to solve the issue next time.

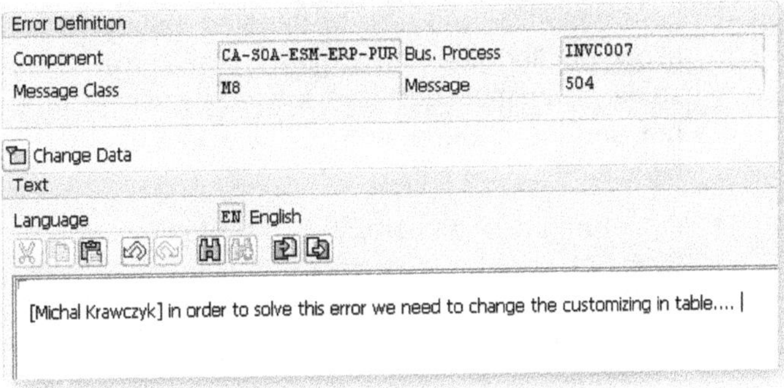

Error Definition
Component
CA-SOA-ESM-ERP-PUR
Bus. Process
INVC007
Message Class
M8
Message
504
Change Data
Text
Language
EN English
[Michal Krawczyk] in order to solve this error we need to change the customizing in table....

Figure 3.15: Hint's information population

Once we save the hint it will always be shown on all of the messages with this particular error.

3.4 Message reprocessing

Every message that ends up in Post Processing Office of Error and Conflict Handler has an error. Therefore, it has to be investigated and its status needs to be changed before the message can be archived (messages with their last status as an error cannot be archived). There are three types of actions that a user can perform on each message as shown in Figure 3.16:

Figure 3.16: Options for error solving

Repeat—if we select this option the system will try to restart the message processing. We can use this option in a few cases:

▶ If a message's content was changed in Post Processing Office and new or updated values should allow posting the message (for example, if the sales order message had a wrong material number and the material number field was updated in ECH's message editor).

▶ If customizing was corrected in a situation where it was not done in a correctly (for example, when posting a sales order with a new sales order type which was not yet transported to the production system).

▶ If an error was only temporary and should not happen anymore (for example, when posting a material master change on a material which is being edited by someone else at the same moment).

Confirm—this options works in two different ways depending on if the SOA integration scenario requires a confirmation or not. If the confirmation for asynchronous scenario is possible using this option, we can inform the sender application that the error was confirmed and no further processing is needed. If the confirmation is not required, then this option will only cancel the error and no further processing is required. Figure 3.17 shows the new entry in the log area of the detailed Error and Conflict Handler screen after using confirm option.

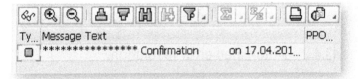

Figure 3.17: Confirm option information

Discard—this option also works in two different ways depending on if the SOA integration scenario requires a confirmation or not. If confirmation for asynchronous scenario is possible using this option, we can inform the sender application about the error by sending the error information. If the confirmation is not required, this option will cancel the error and no further processing is required. Figure 3.18 shows the new entry in the log area of the detailed Error and Conflict Handler screen after using confirm option.

Figure 3.18: Discard option information

3.4.1   Custom specific error processing options

In the event that you are not using SAP standard enterprise services for posting SOA integration scenarios, but a custom build enterprise services, we can freely assign any kind of actions to the three processing options using custom ABAP coding. This can be very useful if different types of IT service management solutions are used like ITIL. In such cases, each of the options can send a message to the IT service processing tool informing it of the action taken.

3.4.2   Automated error resolution

Apart from manual error resolution available from the Postprocessing Office detailed screen, it's also possible to define automated restarting for some specific SOA integration scenarios. Imagine we are posting material master changes and the transaction is locked as another process is doing the same thing at the same moment. In this situation, it's best to assign errors to the automated restarting process of Error and Conflict Handler which is based on Hierarchical Derivation Service. We can call the resolution strategy customizing directly from transaction ech_resol_comp and on the first screen, select the ECH COMPONENT. Depending on which enterprise service we want to use, they can be based on different components. However, for the purpose of the explanation we can select the PURCHASING COMPONENT as shown in Figure 3.19.

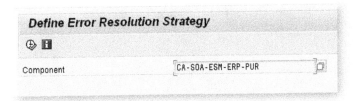

Figure 3.19: Resolution strategy component selection

On the next screen, you can select the condition that specifies when the resolution strategy should take place. The most common condition field is ERROR CATEGORY, but you can also select some other categories (like PRO-CESS NAME). In the next step, you need to define the mode of resolution strategy and we have two modes available:

▶ Persistent mode—In persistent mode, the system immediately creates the Postprocessing Office Order (with error message) after the first try of processing of the message.

▶ Transient mode—In transient mode, the system will first try to solve the error automatically without creating the Postprocessing Office Order (with an error message).

You can combine modes and that would mean that the message resolution strategy will at first try to use the transient mode to solve it and if this is not possible, then it will use the persistent mode to create the Postpro-cessing Office Order. Below you can see the description of the fields for both modes and the actual implementa-tion in Figure 3.20:

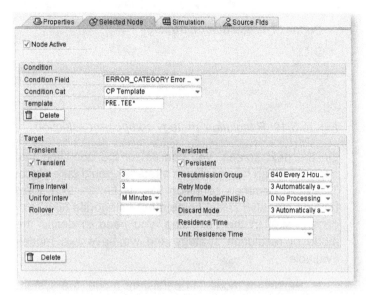

Figure 3.20: Resolution Strategy implementation

Transient mode:

▶ Retry—number of retries.

▶ Time interval—time between the retries (should not be very long).

▶ Unit for internal—unit of measurement for time interval (minutes or hours).

▶ Rollover—time difference between the retries (linear or exponential).

Persistent mode:

▶ Resubmission group—period in which the system executes automated retries.

▶ Retry mode—determines if users are allowed to execute the repeat option manually, or only in the automated mode.

▶ Confirm mode—similar to the retry mode, determines if users are allowed to execute the confirm
option manually, or only in the automated mode.

▶ Discard mode—similar to the retry mode, determines if users are allowed to execute the discard
option manually or only in the automated mode.

▶ Residence time—defined as the interval during
which it's possible to use the repeat button in the
manual mode. After that time, it's only possible to
use the confirm and the discard options.

▶ Unit—residence time—unit of measurement residence time.

After setting up the Resolution Strategy, make sure that
it's saved and activated and you can use it to manage
Postprocessing Office errors in automated mode which
can simplify the monitoring of a SOA integration scenarios.

3.5   Content-based message search

In most cases, it's not enough to be able to select messages on the basis of the SOA integration scenario
header information only (interface name/namespace,
sender/receiver system name, etc.). The Error and Conflict Hander, just like Local Integration Engine Monitor,
allows you to specify which fields of the message payload are searchable on the entry screen of the main
ECH transaction. In order to be able to use fields from
the message for searching, first we need to define the
set of fields we want to use for searching. Next, we will
define those fields as payload attributes in customizing
using the menu path SPRO • CROSS-APPLICATION COM-
PONENTS • PROCESSES AND TOOLS FOR ENTERPRISE APPLI-
CATIONS • ENTERPRISE SERVICES • ERROR AND CONFLICT

HANDLER • DEFINE PAYLOAD ATTRIBUTES. In this example, we will make one field, company code, searchable. As per Figure 3.21 we need to define:

▶ Payload Characteristic—this is freely definable ID of the payload field.

▶ Attribute's Description—In this field, we can define the field description, which will be later visible in the monitoring transaction so you need to make sure the description is clear for all end users.

▶ Structure Name—If we want to be able to use F4 help we need to make sure that we link the payload attribute to the structure that holds the field on the basis of which we want to create the search help.

▶ Field Name—Similarly to the structure name, we also need to specify the field that will be used for search help.

New Entries: Overview of Added Entries

Define Payload Attributes

Payload Characteristic	Attribute Description	Structure name	Field Name
COMPANY_ID	Michal's Company ID	t001	BUKRS

Figure 3.21: Adding a payload attribute

Once the payload attribute is set we need to define payload specific settings in SPRO • CROSS-APPLICATION COMPONENTS • PROCESSES AND TOOLS FOR ENTERPRISE APPLICATIONS • ENTERPRISE SERVICES • ERROR AND CONFLICT HANDLER • DEFINE PAYLOAD SPECIFIC SETTINGS. Payload specific settings are the link between the payload attribute and actual field from the message. In the

initial screen of DEFINE PAYLOAD SPECIFIC SETTINGS we
need to select a few values like business process, component, payload type and DDIC object which can be
taken from the ADDITIONAL DATA SECTION of the Order
details screen of ECH monitoring transaction and from
the MESSAGE DATA display section of the same transaction. In this example, we will add payload specific settings to the SAP standard enterprise service InvoiceER-
PRequest_In. That's why we need to define the values
as shown in Figure 3.22.

Business Process	INVC003
Component	CA-SOA-ESM-ERP-PUR
Payload Type	POST
DDIC Object	IVE_E_INVOICE_ERP_REQUEST

Figure 3.22: Defining payload specific settings

On the next screen, we need to add the new attribute
and select the one defined in payload attributes customizing section and drag and drop the field name from the
left hand side of the screen to extraction path of the attribute as shown in Figure 3.23.

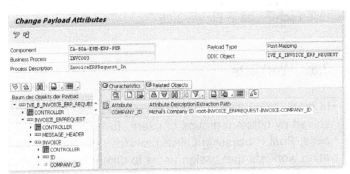

*Figure 3.23: Assigning a message field to the payload
attribute*

Once a new message is processed, we can select the appropriate payload attribute in the payload characteristic field of the initial screen of ECH monitoring transaction. If the attribute was defined with F4 search help correctly, then we can use the search help to populate the extracted value section as shown in Figure 3.24.

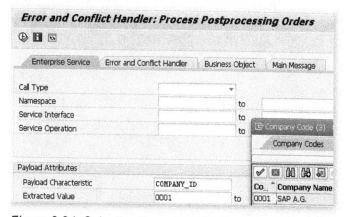

Figure 3.24: Selecting the values for Payload Attributes

If the search was successful, then we will only see messages that have values specified in the entry screen and we can also see all payload attributes in the PAYLOAD ATTRIBUTES section of the MESSAGE DATA part of the detailed screen as in Figure 3.25.

3.6 Worklists

In many companies different error types may need to be solved by different groups of users. To facilitate this process, Post Processing Office provides the option of creating worklists that assign users to different components that are always assigned to specific enterprise services. In this manner, every user can immediately display only those errors which he or she can solve. In order to create a new worklist, we need to open customizing SPRO • CROSS-APPLICATION COMPONENTS • PROCESSES AND TOOLS FOR ENTERPRISE APPLICATIONS • ENTERPRISE SERVICES • ERROR AND CONFLICT HANDLER • POSTPROCESSING OFFICE • WORKLIST • DEFINE WORKLISTS. We need to select the component and worklist's name as shown in Figure 3.26.

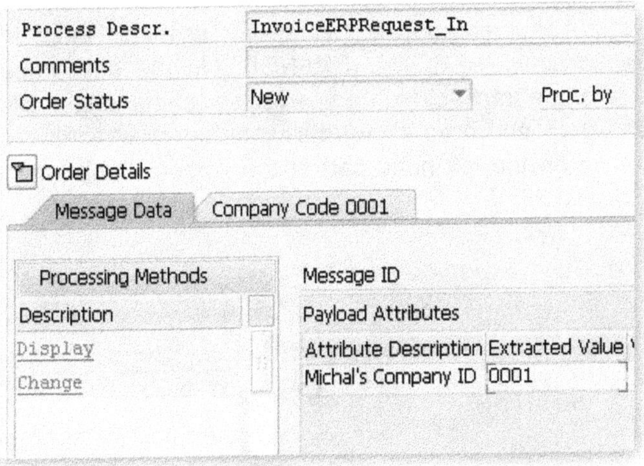

Figure 3.25: Payload attributes in the detailed ECH monitoring screen

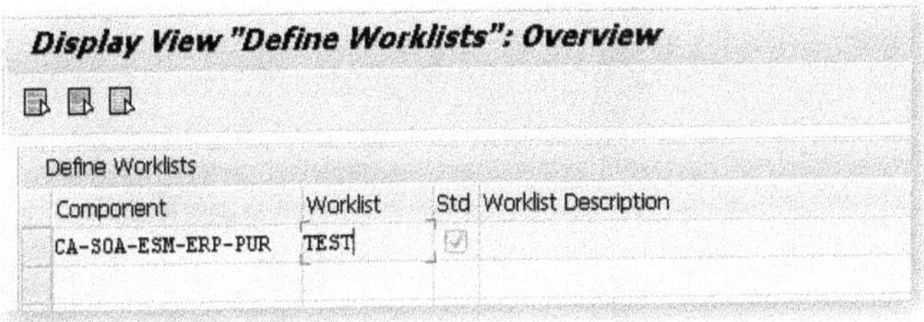

Figure 3.26: Worklist creation

It's also possible to define the worklist as a standard worklist (see standard worklist checkbox in Figure 3.26). Doing so means that if the system cannot find any other worklist assigned to the Postprocessing Order message, then the standard list would be assigned. It's also possible to assign the worklist to an Error and Conflict Handler Business Process to even further subdivide different worklists, but it's not a mandatory configuration and we won't go into further detail on the topic here. Once the worklist is created, we can assign users to them in transaction /SAPPO/WL_CHANGE. On the right hand side of the transaction, we need to select the USER NAME and drag and drop it into the WORKLIST NAME which is visible on the left hand part of the screen as shown in Figure 3.27.

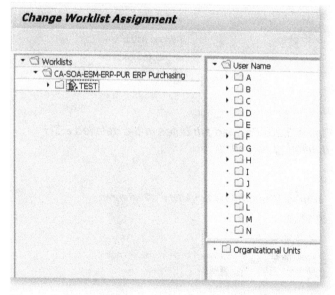

Figure 3.27: Assigning users to the worklist

If the assignment is done and new messages were created in the Postprocessing Office, we can open ECH monitoring transaction ECH_MONI_SEL. In the technical settings section, there is a field called ORDER ASSIGN-MENT, which by default is populated with value ORDERS IN MY WORKLIST as per Figure 3.28. After we run the selection, only messages assigned to the worklist should be displayed, which in many cases can eliminate entering any other filtering criteria by the responsible user.

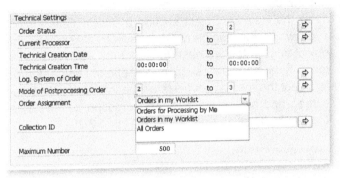

Figure 3.28: Order assignment in the ECH monitoring transaction

3.7   Object linking

Some fields of the inbound messages can contain data which exists in target system. A typical example of those values are master data values like material numbers, customer/vendor numbers, or transactional data like contract numbers. Sometimes users that monitor messages in Error and Conflict Handler would like to be able to navigate directly from the message monitoring transaction to the object display transactions of the SAP backend application system without needing to open new transactions in new sessions. Error and Conflict Hander provides the option of assigning message values to different transactions which can be opened directly from the ECH monitoring screen. In the following example, we will display the object Company Code from the monitoring screen. In order to do that, we need to define payload specific settings in the customizing SPRO • CROSS-APPLICATION COMPONENTS • PROCESSES AND TOOLS FOR ENTERPRISE APPLICATIONS • ENTERPRISE SERVICES • ERROR AND CONFLICT HANDLER • DEFINE PAYLOAD SPECIFIC SETTINGS in a similar way as described in Section 3.5 on content-based message search. Next, we will open the Related Object section and select the Object Type which for Company Code is BUS0002. Once the object is selected we need to select the KEY FIELDS button and the key fields section will appear. Drag and drop to select the message's fields on the left hand side of the screen and assign them to the extraction path fields of the key fields section as shown in Figure 3.29.

Figure 3.29: Assigning message values to the related objects

Once the assignment is complete, every new message in the monitoring screen should contain an additional tab in the ORDER DETAILS section as shown in Figure 3.30.

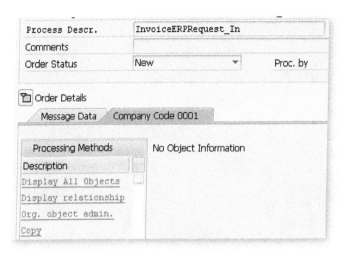

Figure 3.30: Related object display in the ECH monitoring screen

This new tab contains all methods which are available for the business object in standard, so in most cases we would be able to have a display method that allows navigating to the object from the ECH monitoring screen.

4 SAP Application Interface Framework

SAP Application Interface Framework (AIF) is an additional, powerful component designed by SAP to facilitate both implementing new SOA integration scenarios, as well as monitoring them. Its functionality can fully replace both the Local Integration Engine monitor, as well as Error and Conflict Handler.

4.1 Activation and initial configuration

From a technical point of view, AIF is installed as a separate ABAP Add-on on ABAP-based backend application systems (ECC, CRM, etc.) and requires an additional license.

> **Important OSS note**
>
> In order to be able to best monitor SOA integration scenarios, ensure that SAP Note 1799544—„Support of Enterprise Services and existing proxy interfaces" is implemented on your the system.

There are two ways to call AIF for an inbound SOA integration scenario:

▶ With the enabler—instead of calling either the BAPI or any other function module for processing the inbound request, we need to call the AIF's module which will later call the original function module.

▶ Without the enabler it's possible to hook AIF monitor into any inbound SOA integration scenario, but with limited functionality (no runtime features available).

Before we can start working with AIF, we need to complete the following initial configuration steps:

▶ Define error handling applications (set up AIF as a standard error handling application for the Application Interface Framework) and set up AIF's monitoring screens during this initial configuration.

▶ Define trace levels.

We can either do this step manually, as described in the section below, or we can copy the predelivered customizing from client 000 with transaction SCC1.

Application ID	AIF
Maintain Application	
Short description	AIF Application
Table of Maintaining Appl. Key Fields	/AIF/T_INF_TBL
Entry Data Facade	/AIF/CL_AIF_ENTRY_DATA_FACADE
Module	/AIF/SAPLAIF_SP_SSC
Screen Number	9101
Appl. Log Context Structure Name	/AIF/BAL_CONTEXT
Action Handler	/AIF/CL_AIF_ACTION_HANDLER
Program Name	
GUI Status	
URL for Interface Monitor	
Image Object Name for Interface Monitor	/AIF/SAP_NETWEAVER_MONITOR

Figure 4.1: Defining the standard error handling application

Define the new error application with transaction /AIF/CUST • Error Handling • Define Applications. If the AIF application does not exist, we need to create it by populating fields according to Figure 4.1.

Once the application is defined, the second step in the same transaction is to Maintain the Application Specific Key Fields for AIF application as shown in Figure 4.2.

The last step in this transaction is to register functions for AIF application in the Register Functions option. Again, we need to populate the standard values as shown in Figure 4.3.

Application ID			AIF	
Maintain Application Specific Key Fields				
P..	Work Fi...	Field Name	Data element	Field Is Sel...
1	P_NS	NS	/AIF/NS	☐
2	S_IFNAME	IFNAME	/AIF/IFNAME	☑
3	P_IFVERS	IFVER	/AIF/IFVERSION	☐

Figure 4.2: Specific Key Fields maintenance application

Application ID				AIF	
Register Functions					
Function	V S...	Butt...	Button Tooltip	Icon	Method Name
CANCEL	1 2	Cancel	Cancel	@3J@	ON_CANCEL_1
MONI	1 3		Integration Engine: Monitor	@16@	ON_MONI_1
QRFC	1 4		QRFC Monitor	@6P@	ON_QRFC_1
RESTART	1 1	Restart	Restart	@15@	ON_RESTART_1
SLOGS	3 1		Display Error Messge(s)	@DR@	ON_SLOGS_3
TRACELEV	1 5		Maintain Trace Level	@4H@	ON_TRACELEV_1

Figure 4.3: Registered function maintenance

71

The second initial configuration step is to define the trace levels with transaction /AIF/CUST • ERROR HANDLING • GLOBAL FEATURES. Trace levels define the level of detail in the log messages, which are saved when AIF is processing messages. You need to define at least trace levels for the lowest trace level (0) as settings will be used by higher trace levels too by default. Trace level 0 is also used in the following cases:

▶ No trace level is defined for the AIF interface.

▶ No trace level was defined for message used in SAP Process Orchestration, or the trace level is expired.

▶ Message was reprocessed, but not via any of the AIF transactions.

When you select the trace level that you want to define the details for, you can define separate entries for trace levels depending on whether the message source is from the framework, or from individual interfaces as shown in Figure 4.4.

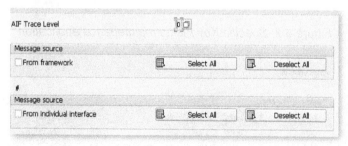

Figure 4.4: Select the appropriate message source

After you select the appropriate message source, you can select what types of predefined message categories should be reported with different levels of five standard message types as shown in Table 4.1:

Message Type	Description
A	Technical Error
E	Application Error
I	Information
W	Warning
S	Success

Table 4.1: Message types used in trace level maintenance

A typical customizing configures the following trace levels:

▶ Trace level 0 only captures application and technical errors.

▶ Trace level 1 includes warning messages.

▶ Trace level 2 includes success messages.

▶ Trace level 3 includes information messages.

A sample configuration for trace level 0 is shown in Figure 4.5.

| AIF Trace Level | | 0 | | |

Message source

☑ From framework   🔲 Select All   🔲 Deselect All

Message Category	Message Type				
#	A	E	I	W	S
(All Categories)	☑	☑	☐	☐	☐
Action (A)	☑	☑	☐	☐	☐
Functions (F)	☑	☑	☐	☐	☐
Value Mappings (V)	☑	☑	☐	☐	☐
Checks (C)	☑	☑	☐	☐	☐
Action Checks (AC)	☑	☑	☐	☐	☐
Mapping Checks (MC)	☑	☑	☐	☐	☐
Interface-sp. func.(IF)	☑	☑	☐	☐	☐
Action-Init func. (AI)	☑	☑	☐	☐	☐
Others (O)	☑	☑	☐	☐	☐
Function errors (FE)	☑	☑	☐	☐	☐
Condition errors (CO)	☑	☑	☐	☐	☐
Alert (AL)	☑	☑	☐	☐	☐

Figure 4.5: Trace configuration

As the primary reason for this book is to describe the monitoring capabilities of AIF, we will not go into the details of AIF design time features. Rather, we will concentrate on customizing the monitoring features only. For that reason, we will start with enabling the AIF monitor for a standard SAP enterprise service. In order to start monitoring an enterprise service in AIF, we need to create two objects:

▶ Namespace—a placeholder used for structuring the objects (for example one namespace for financial interfaces, another one for logistics, etc. Alternatively, you can create two groups—one for inbound and another one for outbound interfaces).

▶ Interface—the main object used in AIF and corresponds with the enterprise service.

To create a new namespace in AIF, we need to go to transaction /AIF/CUST/ • INTERFACE DEVELOPMENT • DEFINE NAMESPACE. Then, we need to create a new entry by selecting the NEW ENTRIES button and inserting the namespace and its description as shown in Figure 4.6.

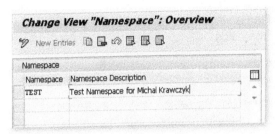

Figure 4.6: Defining a namespace for an AIF interface

Before we can create an AIF interface, we need to know the name of the inbound class of the enterprise service. We can find the name when we open the inbound enterprise service which we want to use in transaction SPROXY. Select the appropriate namespace where the service is located and double-click on its name. Once we do that, we can get the name of the proxy class from the PROPERTIES tab from the IMPLEMENTING CLASS field as shown in Figure 4.7.

Service Provider				FlightBookingOrderRequest_In	Active
Properties	External View	Internal View	Used Objects	Configuration	WSDL

External Key

Type	Service Interface	▼ Source	Enterprise Service Repos
Name	FlightBookingOrderRequest_In		
Namespace	http://sap.com/xi/XI/Demo/Airline		

Proxy

Proxy Name	II_SXIDAL_FBO_REQUEST	Prefix	SXIDAL_
Implementing Class	CL_SXIDAL_FBO_REQUEST		
WebService Definition	SXIDAL_FBO_REQUEST		

Figure 4.7: Finding the name of the proxy class

75

Now that we have the name of the inbound proxy class, we can create an AIF interface in transaction /AIF/CUST/ • INTERFACE DEVELOPMENT • DEFINE INTERFACES. First, we need to select the namespace created in the previous step. Then, we need to select the NEW ENTRIES button. From there, we can define all of the AIF interface details. For generating an inbound AIF interface, we only need to populate three fields:

▶ Interface name—a 10 character AIF interface name.

▶ Interface version—each interface can either have one or multiple runtime versions and each interface is always defined by three objects: namespace, interface name, and interface version.

▶ Proxy class Inbound—this is the name of the inbound class which processes the enterprise service (can be populated using the F4 button search help).

Once we confirm the required entries by clicking the ENTER button, the system will prepopulate some other fields like Raw Data Structure and Records Type in Raw Structure as shown in Figure 4.8.

The other fields that you can populate for the AIF interface are:

▶ Description—a short description of the interface.

▶ SAP Data Structure—this is the structure that is used by AIF for transferring data to function modules in case of inbound interfaces, or from function modules in case of outbound interfaces.

▶ Raw Data Structure—this is the generated ABAP proxy structure.

Figure 4.8: AIF interface definition

▶ Record Type in Raw Data Structure—main component of the Raw Data Structure.

▶ Move corresponding structures—you can select this checkbox if the source and target data structures are similar and you want to transfer the data between them automatically.

▶ Check function module—this is a place for a function module, which will be executed after the AIF mapping and before the execution of any actions (processing step in AIF).

▶ Init Function module before Mapping—this is a place for a function module, which will be executed before the AIF mapping.

▶ Init Function module before Processing—this is a place for a function module, which will be executed after the AIF mapping.

- ▶ Separate Commit—specifies if a separate commit work statement needs to be executed after the AIF interface is processed.

- ▶ Lifetime application log—number of days after which SLG1 logs generated during processing of the interface can be removed.

- ▶ Test mode—if you don't want to do database commit for the interface you can specify it to run in the test mode.

- ▶ Proxy class Outbound—this is the name of the generated outbound proxy class.

- ▶ Field for sending system—if you want to process different AIF mappings depending on the system name, you can specify a field that contains the system name. This name can be used later on to separate message processing.

- ▶ Status Handling—you can also specify the status of the interface (development, test, production, obsolete). If the automated client control is set, this status will be checked against the role of the SAP backend application system.

- ▶ End Date –if the status of the interface is set to obsolete and the end date is greater than the current date message processing for this interface will be stopped with an error message.

If the minimal configuration with required fields for the interface set up was done, it's possible to use the AIF monitoring transaction to start monitoring the SOA Integration flow.

4.2 Additional configuration for Interface Monitor

In order to be able to use an additional monitor called Interface Monitor, which provides a personalized overview of interfaces, we need to perform a few additional customizing steps. Interface Monitor is a tool that gathers alerts that you can assign a specific user to. That's why the customizing needs to start with a definition of an alert recipient. We can define the alert recipient in two locations:

▶ Namespace level—in the event that you want to have one alert recipient for all interfaces under one namespace.

▶ Interface level—in the event that you want separate monitoring of interfaces defined under one namespace.

If we want to define alert recipient on the namespace level, we need to open transaction /AIF/CUST/ • ERROR HANDLING • NAMESPACE SPECIFIC FEATURES, select the namespace and under the node DEFINE RECIPIENTS and create a NEW ENTRY with the new recipient's name and a short description. Alternatively, we can define a URL with error related information as shown in Figure 4.9.

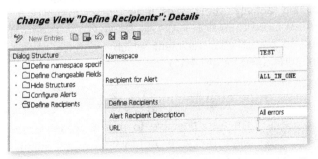

Figure 4.9: Namespace specific recipient determination

Alternatively, if we'd like to define an alert recipient on the namespace level we need to open transaction /AIF/CUST/ • ERROR HANDLING • INTERFACE SPECIFIC FEATURES. Select the interface and namespace on the selection screen and create a NEW ENTRY under the node ASSIGN RECIPIENTS WITHOUT KEY FIELDS where you need to specify the namespace and RECIPIENT NAME as shown in Figure 4.10.

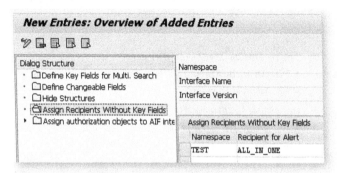

Figure 4.10: Interface specific recipient determination

After the alert recipient is defined, we need to assign either users or user groups to the recipient. It's also possible to define external addresses where the alerts can be forwarded, but for the purpose of the Interface Monitor we will only show how to assign single users. Customizing activity starts with transaction /AIF/CUST/ • SYSTEM CONFIGURATION • ASSIGN RECIPIENTS. Then you need to select your recipient which we have already configured (see Figure 4.11).

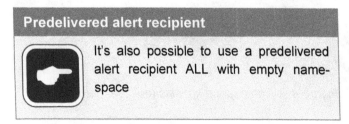

Predelivered alert recipient

It's also possible to use a predelivered alert recipient ALL with empty namespace

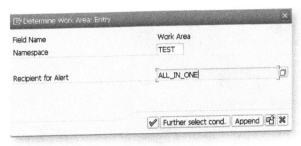

Figure 4.11: Customizing the alert recipients

If we want to assign a user to the alert recipient we need to create NEW ENTRIES under the ASSIGN USERS node and define:

▶ User name—name of the user who will be responsible for monitoring that particular interface (for interface specific alert recipients), or a group of interfaces (for namespace specific alert recipients).

▶ Message type—defines which types of messages will be displayed in the interface monitoring transaction which includes: application error or technical error messages, information messages, success messages, warning messages, application error messages, technical error messages, and none.

▶ Include in Overview screen—this checkbox specifies if the alert should be displayed in the Overview screen of the Interface Monitor transaction.

▶ Technical User—this checkbox specifies if the user will be allowed to monitor messages in a technical error.

Sample settings for user assignment for the alert recipient are shown in Figure 4.12 where two message types are defined for monitoring.

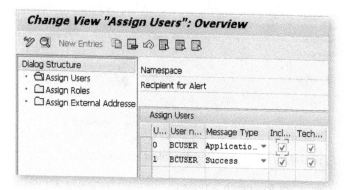

Figure 4.12: User assignment for the alert recipient

You can define different message types for different users in cases where one interface needs to be monitored by different users. For example, one business user monitoring the interface for application errors only and another one monitoring the same interface for technical errors only.

4.3 Interface Monitor

AIF provides two applications for users that are responsible for handling SOA integration monitoring. Interface Monitor is a tool you can use to get an overview of all interfaces assigned to a particular user (see section 4.2 for information on user assignment). Once this configuration is complete, there are two ways (two transactions) to open the Interface monitor application:

▶ /AIF/IFMON—this transaction opens the application in SAP GUI.

▶ /AIFX/ERR_WEB—this transaction opens the web based Interface Monitor.

Once you open either of those transactions you see the calendar (see Figure 4.13). In this case, it is the SAP GUI version where you can select which dates you want to monitor and note that the monitor will refresh automatically.

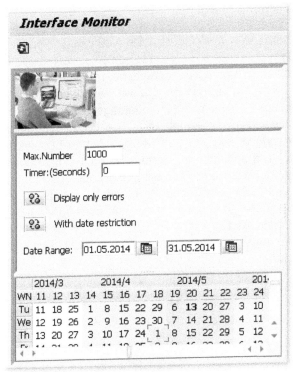

Figure 4.13: Calendar view of the Interface Monitor for SAP GUI-based application

The calendar also gives you initial insight into the status of messages as days are marked with different colors depending on the status of messages. The message color coding is as follows:

▶ Red: There is at least one message that resulted in an error.

▶ Yellow: There are messages with warnings, but there are no messages with errors.

▶ Green: There are only correctly processed messages for that day.

In the same view (see Figure 4.13), you can also specify how many messages you want to see (MAXIMUM NUMBER) and how the transaction should be refreshed (TIMER: SECONDS). The last option (Timer) seems to be very simple, but it gives a huge advantage over any other SOA Integration monitoring tools like Local Integration Engine monitor or Error and Conflict Hander because it allows for a monitoring interface without any manual actions. It's possible to have this transaction open for the entire day (even on a separate monitor), in order to be able to see the status of all of the interfaces very quickly. The second part of the Integration Monitor, apart from the calendar view, is the Message Overview as shown in Figure 4.14.

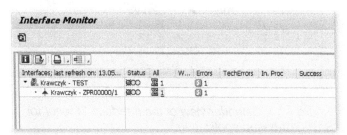

Figure 4.14: Calendar view of the Interface Monitor for a SAP GUI-based application

Message overview gives you an overview of all interfaces grouped by the namespace. If you open the namespace level, you can see the summary of the messages on the interface level. For each status, the total number of messages is displayed. Apart from standard red, yellow, and green statuses (similar to those in the calendar view) which can you can see in the status column, there's also a set of statuses visible under the rest of the grouping columns. They are:

▶ Warnings—Indicates how many messages have a warning status.

▶ Application errors—Indicates how many messages have application errors.

▶ Successfully processed—shows how many messages we processed correctly.

▶ Cancelled messages—shows how many messages were cancelled.

▶ Technical error—shows how many messages have a technical error. This status is only visible if your user was defined as a technical user in Interface Monitoring customization.

▶ In process—shows how many messages have an in process status. This status is also only visible if your user was defined as a technical user in Interface Monitoring customization.

Interface Monitor has a set of other functions that can be used to obtain more details about a specific interface. If you select the INTERFACE INFORMATION button (see icon with I in Figure 4.14) you can display the documentation maintained for the interface. If you use the MESSAGE SUMMARY button (placed next to the information button), then the transaction will display a detailed list of messages that are related to the selected interface as shown in Figure 4.15.

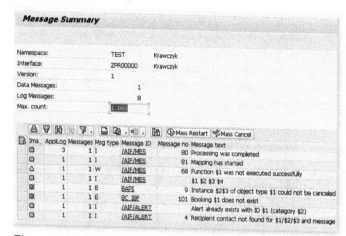

Figure 4.15: Message summary for a SAP GUI-based application

A similar set of functions is also available for the web based transaction (see Figure 4.16).

Figure 4.16: Interface Monitor for a web-based application

For both types of Interface Monitor applications, we also have one additional function. When we select the number of messages in any of the columns where the number is displayed, the transaction will automatically start the second monitoring transaction—Monitoring and Error Handling with the interface selection completed at the Interface Monitor level.

4.4 Message monitoring and error monitoring

Message monitoring and error handling in AIF is mostly done with the use of a second monitoring application available with AIF called Monitoring and Error Handling. This application, similar to the Interface Monitor, is available in SAP GUI and as a web-based transaction.

4.4.1 Monitoring and Error Handling—SAP GUI version

You can start the SAP GUI version of the Monitoring and Error Handling application with transaction /AIF/ERR/. On the first selection screen, you will see a number of selection criteria including:

▶ Application Selection—where you can select the application defined in the initial customizing (see Figure 4.17).

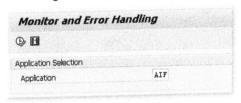

Figure 4.17: Application selection

▶ Application Specific Selection—where you can select your interface namespace, name, version,
and also message class and message number
(Figure 4.18).

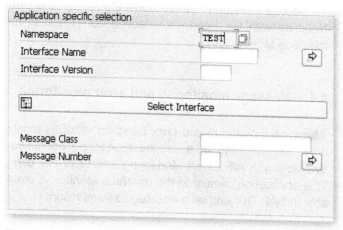

Figure 4.18: Application specific selection

▶ Generic Selection—where you can select the
message creation date, time, and message ID
(see Figure 4.19).

Figure 4.19: Generic selection

▶ Status Selection—where you can select the status
of messages that you want to monitor (see Figure
4.20).

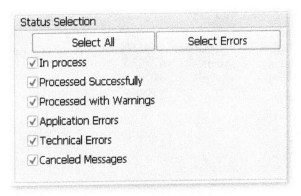

Figure 4.20: Message status selection

▶ Additional Parameters (see Figure 4.21)—where you can select the TECHNICAL VIEW checkbox which displays the additional monitor on the next screen and EMERGENCY CORRECTION checkbox which will make all fields of the message editable independently of all other settings. MAX NUMBER FIELD defines how many messages will be displayed.

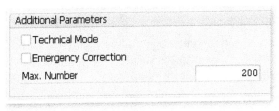

Figure 4.21: Additional parameters selection

After making the appropriate selections on the selection screen the main AIF Error Handling screen will appear. It also consists of several sections:

▶ The data message view as shown in Figure 4.22 displays all messages grouped by namespace, interface name, version, as well as some other criteria like key fields.

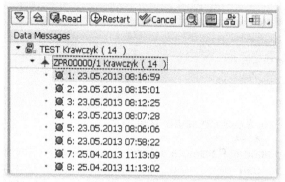

Figure 4.22: Data message view

The data message view toolbar provides multiple functions that work when you select the message:

▶ **Expand and collapse selected nodes**—allows you to display all messages under a specific selection criteria.

▶ **Read**—reading messages allows you to refresh the main screen and populate it only with data for messages selected for reading.

▶ **Restart**—restart allows manual restarting of selected messages or nodes of messages after an error is fixed.

▶ **Cancel**—in the event that a message cannot be restarted and the error was handled in another manner (like manual entry in the transaction) the message can be cancelled. The system will not archive messages which stay in error status and that's why it's important to mark all messages that should not be processed as cancelled.

▸ **Navigate to standard monitor**—this button allows you to navigate from the AIF error monitor to
the original monitor that can be used to process a
message (for example Local Integration Engine
monitor in case of an Enterprise Service message).

▸ **Navigate to qRFC monitor**—you can open the
qRFC monitor with this button.

▸ **Maintain Trace Level**—in case you need any
more information about the processed message
you can change its trace level (increase it) and restart the message. After this action, you should be
able to see more information in the log message
view.

▸ **Change layout**—you can change the layout of the
hierarchical tree in the data message view.

▸ **Log message view**—shows all related log messages that were created during message processing as shown in Figure 4.23.

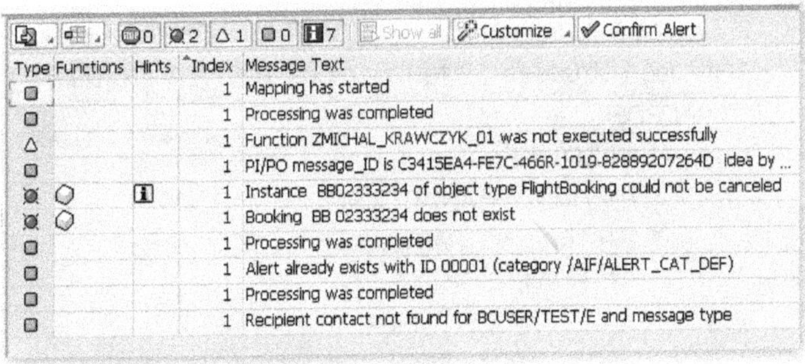

Figure 4.23: Log message view

Functions that can be used with the log message view
include:

▸ **Export**—allows you to export log messages to file
system.

▶ **Choose layout**—you can choose the layout in the log message view.

▶ **Display or hide messages** of a certain type—you can select if you want to see all types of log message or only specific types (for example, errors only).

▶ **Dynamic support in error solving**—AIF provides the option to define additional procedures for supporting error solving which can be attached to specific log messages. We will cover those additional custom hints and custom functions which will be described in the section 4.5.

▶ **Confirm alert**—in case the processing of the message started with an alert, it's possible to confirm this alert in the log message view.

▶ **Data structure view**—shows the structure of the messages selected in the data message view. Structures are made of nested tables and other structures as shown in Figure 4.24.

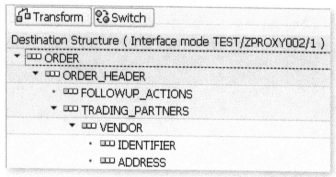

Figure 4.24: Data structure view

You can either display the data in the raw structure or in the SAP structure using the TRANSFORM button. If you double-click on any of the structures, the data content view will be refreshed and data stored in the selected structure will be displayed there.

▶ Data content view—displays the data of the structures selected in the data structure view as shown in Figure 4.25.

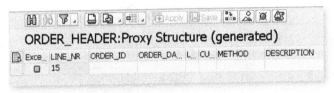

Figure 4.25: Data content view

Additional data content view functions include:

▶ **Field editing**—it's possible to change each field of the message and save a new version of the message before reprocessing it. You can also restrict field editing with authorizations on a field or structure level.

▶ **Find**—with this function, you can search all selected structures for a particular value—this is very useful in situations where you would like to perform a search in all lines of the message at once.

▶ **Filter**—you can filter out some of the lines of the data content view.

▶ **Print**—it's possible to print out the message content.

▶ **Export**—it's also possible to export the message content for a file system.

▶ **Choose layout**—you can choose the layout in the data content view.

▶ **Apply**—to apply all changes in the edited field we can use the apply button.

▶ **Save**—allows saving the values of the edited fields highlighted in yellow.

▶ **Search and Replace**—a function which allows changing multiple fields at once.

▶ **Full screen**—you can open the data content view in the full screen mode. This is very useful when you are comparing data between different messages (for example, one with an error and the other one successful).

▶ **Show error messages**—this button allows you to show the fields that are related to the error messages from the log message view.

▶ **Display error messages**—displays the log messages belonging to a data structure line in the log messages screen.

▶ **Technical view**—if the technical view checkbox was selected on the AIF Error Handing selection screen a fifth selection screen will be visible as shown in Figure 4.26.

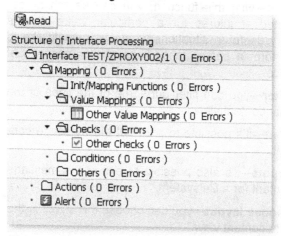

Figure 4.26: Technical view

The technical view displays interface specific steps that are customized for each message processed with AIF and allows deep analysis of each of those steps. For example, you can find all error messages initiated during the mapping step.

4.4.2 Monitoring and Error Handling web-based version

The second version of the Monitoring and Error handling application is available as a web-based application, but it's not possible to open it in a similar way as the SAP GUI version. In order to open the web-based Monitoring and Error handling application, first we need to open the Interface Monitor (transaction /AIFX/ERR_WEB), select the interface that we want to monitor, and navigate to the web-based Monitoring and Error handling application (see Figure 4.27) by selecting the number of messages. For example, under the ALL MESSAGES column to display all messages related to the selected interface.

Figure 4.27: Web-based Monitoring and Error handling application

Both SAP GUI and web-based applications have a similar look and feel as well as a similar set of functions. The main differences between the two applications are:

► Data message view—it's not possible to navigate to other applications like IDOC monitor, Local Integration Engine monitor, nor qRFC monitor from the web-based application.

► Data structure view—the web-based application does not have this view.

The other functions work in exactly the same way for both applications. It is simply a matter of user preference when it comes to which of the two types of applications the user uses.

4.4.3 Automated error processing

SAP introduced automated processing of error messages to AIF with Service Pack 03. As of this Service Pack, it's now possible to generate background jobs that will reprocess the configured failed messages. Administrators can now define not only which error messages should be reprocessed, but also the time intervals and number of retries. Automated error reprocessing settings can be customized in two transactions:

► /AIF/REP_AC_DEF—transaction to define the reprocessing actions which are functions that handle the reposting process.

► /AIF/REP_AC_ASGN—transaction to assign automated reprocessing actions to the interface and error message.

Transaction /AIF/REP_AC_DEF (see Figure 4.28) is used to define the reprocessing action and you can specify the following fields:

▶ **Namespace**—interface namespace.

▶ **Reprocessing Action Name**—AIF delivers one default reprocessing action for automated restart of error messages.

▶ **Function Module**—Function module used for predelivered reprocessing action is /AIF/RESTART_MSG. However, it's possible to create custom modules on the basis of the template function—/AIF/TEMPL_RESTART_AUTO_REPR.

▶ **Runtime Configuration ID**—runtime configuration which can be set up using transaction /AIF/PERS_CGR.

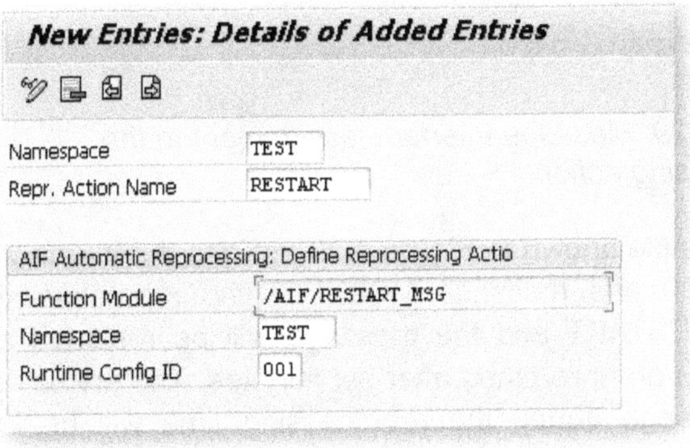

Figure 4.28: AIF reprocessing action setup

In the next step using transaction /AIF/REP_AC_ASGN we can assign a particular error (for example "object locked"—MC601) of a single interface to the reprocessing action as shown in Figure 4.29.

Change View "AIF Automatic Reprocessing: Assign

New Entries

Namespace	TEST
Interface Name	ZPR00000
Interface Version	1
Message ID	MC
Message	601
Namespace	
Recipient for Alert	

AIF Automatic Reprocessing: Assign Reprocessing Action

Namespace	TEST
Repr. Action Name	RESTART
Max Repr. Counter	3
Min. Time in Seconds	
Min. Time in Minute	3
Mim. Time in Hours	
Max. Time in Seconds	
Max. Time in Minutes	6
Max. Time in Hours	
Intermediate Status	In Process

Figure 4.29: Message/interface assignment to the reprocessing action

The example shown in Figure 4.29 assigns the interface ZPR00000 and message MC601 to the reprocessing action RESTART and the message will be restarted a maximum of three times after six minutes. The status of the message during the reprocessing time will be IN PROCESS.

4.5   Hints for error monitoring

In order to attach user notes for some of the error messages, AIF provides functionality for creating hints. In order to create a new hint, we need to open the log message view of the Monitoring and Error Handling transaction (/AIF/ERR/) and select the row in the HINTS column next to the message for which we want to create a hint. This will open a new input screen as shown in Figure 4.30, where you can:

▶ Insert a tooltip—text which will be visible in the log message view of the Monitoring and Error Handling transaction after selecting the error and without going into the details of the hint.

▶ Select the language for the hint.

▶ Insert a descriptive text where you can describe what needs to be done when this error occurs.

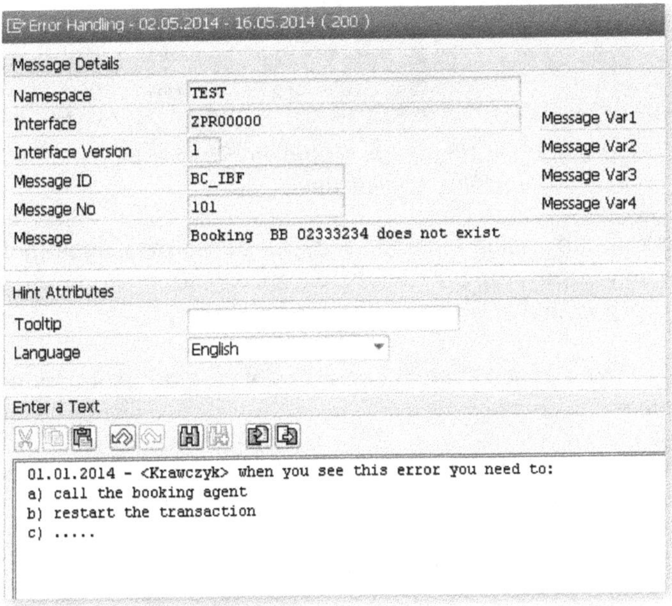

Figure 4.30: Hint creation

After you save the hint, it will be visible each time the same log message appears. For the web-based version of the Monitoring and Error Handling application, you create the hints in a similar way. The only difference is that after you select the message in the log message view you need to select CUSTOMIZE • CUSTOM HINTS • NEW from the main menu area of the log message view as shown in Figure 4.31.

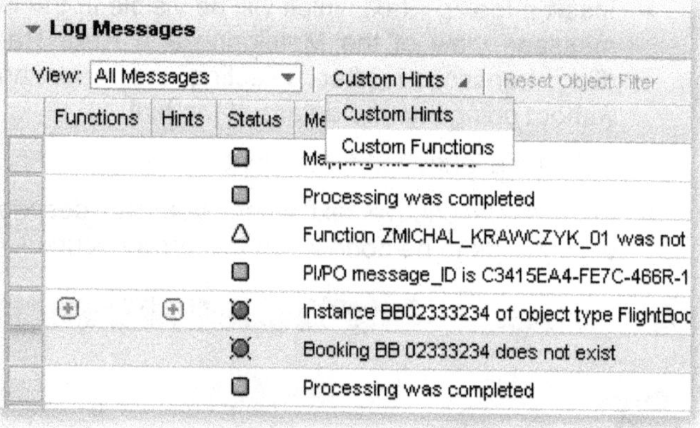

Figure 4.31: Hint creation on the web-based Monitoring and Error Handling application

You can assign hints for all types of log messages (not only for errors), but it's advisable to create them as often as possible at least for error log messages.

System administrators can also define other hint parameters such as:

▶ Visibility for user—define if the hint is visible for a current user only, for a group of users, or to all users.

▶ Scope/visibility for interfaces/messages—define if the hint is displayed for one interface, or for all interfaces for one or multiple messages.

System administrators can perform this assignment with transaction /AIF/CUST_HINTS as shown in Figure 4.32.

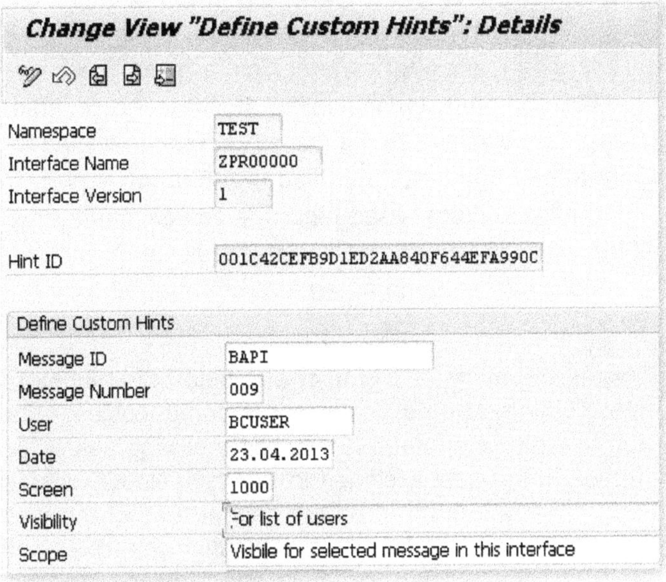

Change View "Define Custom Hints": Details

Namespace	TEST
Interface Name	ZPR00000
Interface Version	1
Hint ID	001C42CEFB9D1ED2AA840F644EFA990C

Define Custom Hints

Message ID	BAPI
Message Number	009
User	BCUSER
Date	23.04.2013
Screen	1000
Visibility	For list of users
Scope	Visbile for selected message in this interface

Figure 4.32: Select the scope and visibility of the hints

4.6 Content-based message search

Monitoring and Error Handling application's entry view allows selecting messages on the basis of different technical message related criteria. In case we need to do message selection on the basis of the values from the content of the message, we need to configure an AIF content-based message search. Content-based message search within AIF can be customized by using key fields.

Key fields

 Key fields in AIF are fields related to the content of the messages, which are particularly important for a given message (like order number for messages related to orders and invoice number for messages related to invoices). Key fields are used in AIF in many places including content-based message search, structuring the views in Error and Conflict Handler, and authorizations (just to name a few).

Key fields are stored in special tables called index tables. That is why it's necessary to create custom index tables which are later used for the message search selection. If the field assigned to the key field can appear only once (for example on the header level of the message), then we need to create a single index table. If the field assigned to the key field can appear more than once (for example, on the line level of the message) we have to create a multiple index table. The configuration required to set up the content-based message search can be divided into four steps:

▶ Create an index table.

▶ Implement a subscreen with the key fields.

▶ Assign the index table and selection subscreen to the interface.

▶ Assign the key fields to the interface fields.

Two of the configuration steps (creating an index table and implementing a subscreen with key fields) require a developer key and basic ABAP development knowledge. The other two steps are typical customization only.

4.6.1 Index table creation

The index table will store the key field values of the messages, that's why prior to defining a new index table it's necessary to determine which field or fields we need to monitor and the level of the field in the messages (header or line item). In this example, we will be monitoring a single field—airline code—of the message that cancels a flight booking. The field can only be used once per message. If the field can appear only once in the message, we need to create a single index table. We can create the table in transaction SE11 and we can start by copying an AIF template table /AIF/STD_IDX_TBL. In order for AIF runtime to be able to select key fields for specific messages from the index table, the custom index table needs to store some of the message identifiers like message GUID. The additional field is the field key which needs to reference the field from the message. For the purpose of this example, we need to add the key field which will reference the airline code field as shown in Figure 4.33.

Field	Key	Ini...	Data element	Data ...	Length	Deci...	Short Description
MANDT	✓	✓	MANDT	CLNT	3	0	Client
MSGGUID	✓	✓	GUID_32	CHAR	32	0	GUID in 'CHAR' For
KEY_FIELD_1			S_CARR_ID	CHAR	3	0	Airline Code
.INCLUDE			/AIF/IFKEYS	STRU	0	0	Keys
.INCLUDE			/AIF/ADMIN	STRU	0	0	Additional informat
PID			SXMSPID	CHAR	40	0	Integration Engine

Figure 4.33: Single index table creation

It's possible to include more than one key field in the table if the content-based message search should use more than one selection field. Once the table is created, we can activate it and use it in subsequent configuration steps.

4.6.2 Key field subscreen implementation

To use the key fields on the entry screen of the Error and Monitoring transaction, you need to create an ABAP subscreen that will include the key fields. The subscreen needs to be implemented as a program type—MODULE POOL, so make sure you select the correct attribute while creating the subselection screen as shown in Figure 4.34.

Title	selection program	
Original language	EN English	
Created	BCUSER	17.05.2014
Last changed by		
Status		

Attributes		
Type	Module Pool	
Status		
Application		
Authorization Group		
Editor lock		✓ Fixed point arithmetic
✓ Unicode Checks Active		

Figure 4.34: Module pool attribute selection

Sample code for the subscreen is shown in Listing 4.1 and the key field for airline code is defined as the P_C2 parameter.

```
PROGRAM ZAIF_TEST_SEL_SCREEN.

SELECTION-SCREEN BEGIN OF SCREEN 0001 AS ↵
SUBSCREEN.
*in this section you need to define your ↵
key field as a parameter (p_c2)
PARAMETERS: p_c2 TYPE string.
SELECTION-SCREEN END OF SCREEN 0001.
AT SELECTION-SCREEN OUTPUT.
/aif/cl_global_tools=>get_value_from_mem( ).
```

Listing 4.1 Module pool code

Before saving and activating the subscreen, we need to make sure that we define the selection texts for the parameters which represent the key field. We can do this by going into the main menu GOTO • TEXT ELEMENTS • SELECTION TEXTS as shown in Figure 4.35.

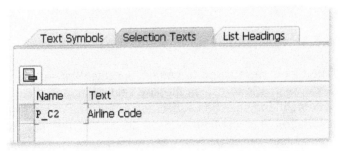

Figure 4.35: Defining the selection texts for key fields

4.6.3 Index table and selection subscreen assignment to the interface

After the index table and subscreen are created, they need to be assigned to the interface on the namespace level with the use of transaction /AIF/CUST/ • ERROR

105

HANDLING • NAMESPACE SPECIFIC FEATURES as shown in Figure 4.36.

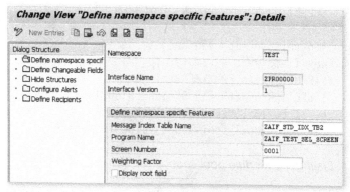

Figure 4.36: Index table assignment to the interface

Apart from the INDEX TABLE name and SUBSELECTION SCREEN name, you also need to define the SCREEN NUMBER of the subselection screen (default 0001).

4.6.4 Key field assignment to the interface

The last step required to configure content-based message search is to assign the key field defined in the index table and selection subscreen to the field of the real interface. This configuration is done with the use of transaction /AIF/CUST/ • ERROR HANDLING •INTERFACE SPECIFIC FEATURES—DEFINE KEY FIELDS FOR MULTI. SEARCH.

Mandatory fields required for setting up the content-based message search include:

▶ Key field name—name of the key field from the index table.

▶ Data element—data element of the key field from the index table.

▶ Name select options/parameter—name of the parameter defined in the subselection screen.

▶ Field name—this field is used to determine which field of the message will be linked to the key field.

▶ Raw or SAP structure—defines if the message field linked to the key field exists in the raw structure, or the SAP structure.

▶ Multiple selection type—determines the scope of the key field (single selection or multiple selection).

Field name definition

 When defining the key field, it's best to define it using the F4 selection and not input the data manually in order to avoid any errors in this section.

Sample customizing for the key field defined in the example defined in this previous chapters is shown in Figure 4.37.

Namespace	TEST
Interface Name	ZPR00000
Interface Version	1
Field Sequence Number	1
General	
Key Field Name	KEY_FIELD_1
Data element	S_CARR_ID
Name Select-Options/Parameter	P_C2
☐ Field Is Select-Option	
☐ Do Not Display as Column	
Weighting Factor	
Field Name	E1SBO_CANC-AIRLINEID
Raw or SAP Structure	Source structure (raw for inbound, SAP for outbound)
Multi.Selection Type	Single selection ▼

Figure 4.37: Key field assignment to the interface field

4.6.5   Content-based search in Error and Monitoring application

Once the setup of the content based message search on the basis of the key fields is finished, you can check the result in the Error and Monitoring transaction—/AIF/ERR. In order to display the custom subscreen with the new searchable field we need to use the SELECT INTERFACE button in the transaction and select the appropriate interface for which the key fields were defined and this will open a new subscreen called MORE SPECIFIC SELECTION where the parameters for the key fields will be available as shown in Figure 4.38.

The index table will store the values of the fields that were processed after the key field was customized. That's why in order to be able to search messages with the use of the new search fields, it's required to run the interface first. It's a good practice to archive the index tables as often as you archive the data for the interface to which the table belongs. Transaction /AIF/IDXTBL (see Figure 4.39) is a transaction that shows the number of entries for index tables and can be used for investigation if the selection takes too much time.

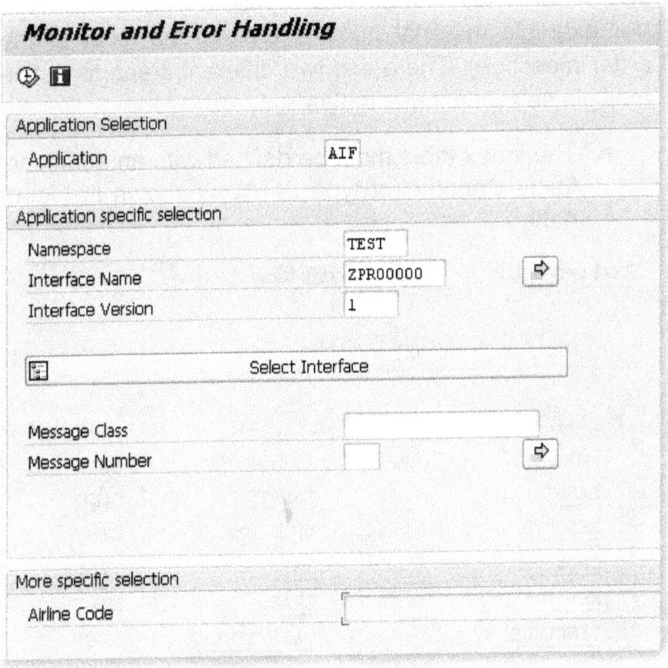

Monitor and Error Handling

⊕ 🟦

Application Selection

Application   `AIF`

Application specific selection

Namespace   `TEST`
Interface Name   `ZPR00000` ⇨
Interface Version   `1`

[⊞]   Select Interface

Message Class
Message Number   ⇨

More specific selection

Airline Code

Figure 4.38: Content-based message search in transaction /AIF/ERR

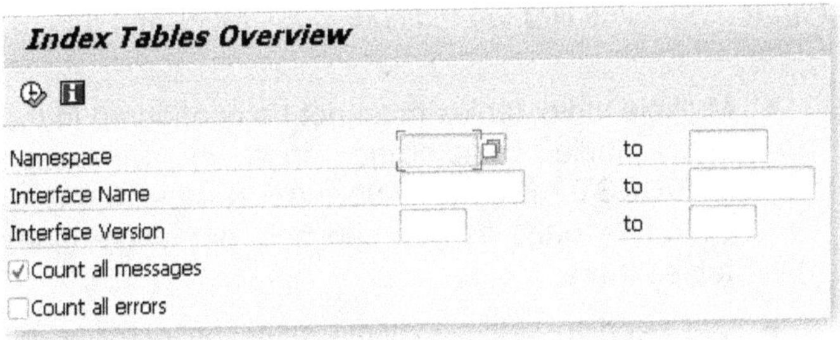

Index Tables Overview

⊕ 🟦

Namespace   [　] to [　]
Interface Name   to
Interface Version   to
☑ Count all messages
☐ Count all errors

Figure 4.39: Index table overview transaction

109

4.6.6   Multiple selection index tables

Customizing multiple selection index tables allows you to search for fields that can be repeated in one message (for example material number on the line level of the order message). There are two different steps to define multiple selection index tables:

▶ The index table must be defined with an additional field—Counter (of type INT4) as shown in Figure 4.40.

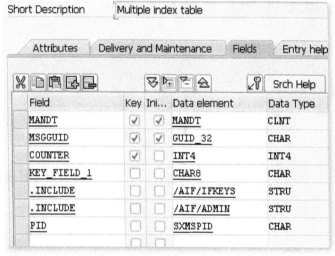

Short Description			Multiple index table	

Attributes	Delivery and Maintenance	Fields	Entry help

Field	Key	Ini...	Data element	Data Type
MANDT	✓	✓	MANDT	CLNT
MSGGUID	✓	✓	GUID_32	CHAR
COUNTER	✓	☐	INT4	INT4
KEY_FIELD_1	☐	☐	CHAR8	CHAR
.INCLUDE	☐	☐	/AIF/IFKEYS	STRU
.INCLUDE	☐	☐	/AIF/ADMIN	STRU
PID	☐	☐	SXMSPID	CHAR

Figure 4.40: Defining the multiple index table with the COUNTER *field*

▶ Multiple index tables must not be configured in the index table customizing done in transaction /AIF/CUST • ERROR HANDLING • NAMESPACE SPECIFIC FEATURES as you can only put single index tables there.

▶ We need to select multiple selection entry in the multiple selection type field in transaction /AIF/CUST • ERROR HANDLING • INTERFACE SPECIF-

IC FEATURES and populate the multiple index table name field with the name of the multiple index table name as shown in Figure 4.41.

Namespace	TEST
Interface Name	ZPR00000
Interface Version	1
Field Sequence Number	1
General	
Key Field Name	KEY_FIELD_1
Data element	CHAR2
Name Select-Options/Parameter	P_C2
☐ Field Is Select-Option	
☐ Do Not Display as Column	
Weighting Factor	
Field Name	E1SBO_CANC-AIRLINEID
Raw or SAP Structure	Source structure (raw for inbound, SAP for outbound)
Multi.Selection Type	Multiple selection ▼
Multiple Selection	
Message Index Table Name	Z_MULTI_INDEX_TAB

Figure 4.41: Interface-specific customizing of the multiple index table

Once this setup is complete, it's possible to use the Monitor and Error Handling transaction to search for fields that exist multiple times in one message.

4.7 Object linking

With AIF, you can customize navigation from the log message view of the Monitor and Error Handling applications in order to decrease the time necessary to performing different checks. A typical case is that we receive an error message because the master data is not maintained (for example no EAN code in a material master). In order to check it, we would need to open the message content on the data content view of the Error and Monitoring application, get the number of the object, open a new session with master data maintenance transaction, and check if the respective value is there or not. With AIF, we don't need to perform all of those steps because it's possible to simply customize a link to the application and it's as simple as creating a new hint for an error message. Customizing the links in AIF is done with the use of functions and in order to create a new function, we need to open the log message view of the Monitoring and Error Handling transaction (/AIF/ERR/) and select the row in the FUNCTIONS column next to the message that we want to create a link for. This will open a new input screen as shown in Figure 4.42.

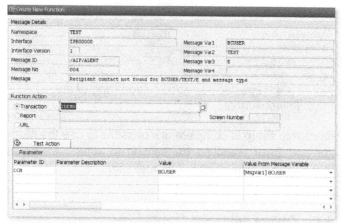

Figure 4.42: Custom function creation

We can create three types of links:

▶ Transaction—link will open a transaction.

▶ Report—link will open an ABAP report.

▶ URL– link will open a URL in the browser.

The most typical type of link is a transaction. In most cases, we may want to view the data (to check if it exists) and for that we need to populate the fields of the entry screen for the transaction. We can populate the entry fields of transactions using parameters available in many of them. When creating a custom function, it's possible to specify a Parameter ID field of the transaction either as a static or a dynamic (with the use of the message variables) value. This way when the transaction is opened, there is no need to insert any values because they are already prepopulated. It is possible to use the Test Action button to test to see if the link is working directly from the customizing screen. Some other customizing attributes of the function as shown in Figure 4.43 include:

▶ Text—custom description of the function.

▶ Tooltip—short description which will be visible in the log message view of the Monitoring and Error Handling transaction after selecting the error and without opening the function.

▶ Language.

▶ Icon—it's possible to select the icon which will be visible in the log message view of the Monitoring and Error Handling transaction next to the error message.

▶ Skip first screen—if a link to a report or a transaction is created, sometimes it's not necessary to see the selection screen (prepopulated with the values from the message variables) and this checkbox allows you to skip it.

▶ In new session—after selecting this checkbox the link to the transaction or report will be opened in a new session.

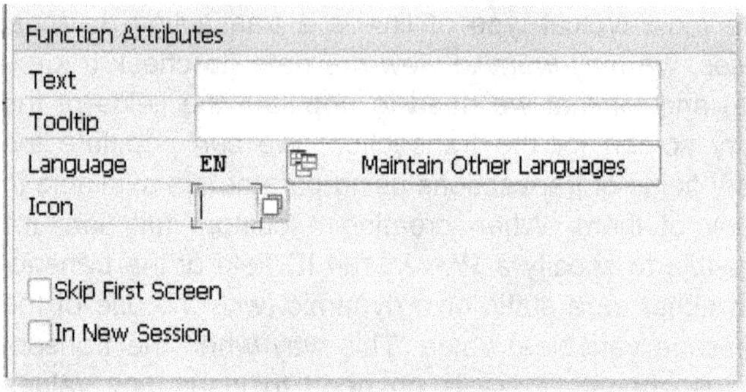

Figure 4.43: Further customizing function attributes

For the web-based version of the Monitoring and Error Handling application, you create the functions in a similar way. The only difference is that after you select the message in the log message view you need to select CUSTOMIZE • CUSTOM FUNCTIONS • NEW from the main menu area of the log message view as shown in Figure 4.44.

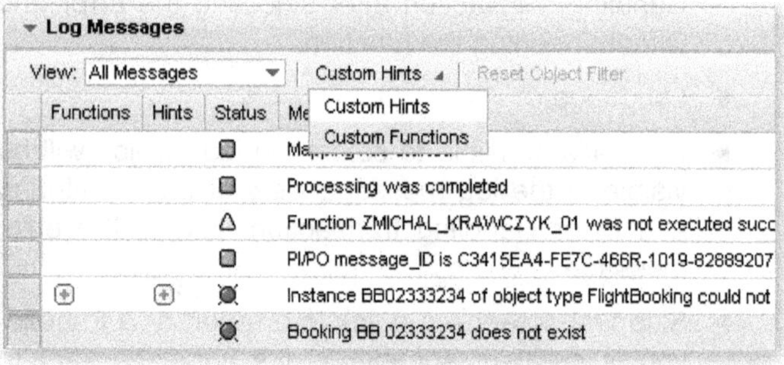

Figure 4.44: Function creation on the web-based Monitoring and Error Handling application

Similarly to the AIF hint's maintenance, system administrators can also define some other function parameters such as:

▶ Visibility for the user—define if the function is visible for a current user only, for a group of users or to all users.

▶ Scope/visibility for interfaces/messages—define if the function is displayed for one interface or for all interfaces for one or multiple messages.

System administrators can perform this assignment with transaction /AIF/CUST_FUNC as shown in Figure 4.45.

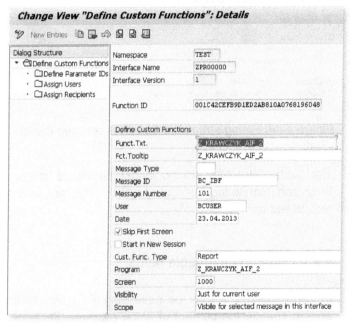

Figure 4.45: Selecting the scope and visibility of custom functions

4.8 Hiding structures

In some cases, the users should not be able to view some parts of the messages like employee payroll information or pricing conditions. AIF provides the option to hide single structures with the use of customizing. In order to hide a structure, open transaction /AIF/CUST • ERROR HANDLING • INTERFACE SPECIFIC FEATURES and select the HIDE STRUCTURES node. Next, you need to create a new entry and in the STRUCTURE TO BE HIDDEN field. Select the structure that should not be displayed in the monitoring transactions as shown in Figure 4.46.

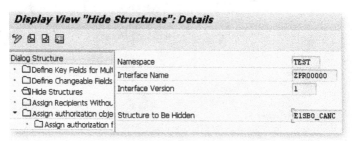

Figure 4.46: Hiding structures from the message display view

The hidden structure will no longer be visible in both Error and Monitoring applications SAP GUI, nor in the web-based applications.

4.9 Defining changable fields

In certain cases, it may be necessary for users to be able to change the content of some message fields before reprocessing them in cases where they were not processed successfully. The default setting in AIF does not allow you to change the content of any fields, but it's possible to change the standard behavior with customizing. This setting can be either done on the namespace level, for all messages within the AIF namespace, or in the interface level when only one interface should be affected. To add a new changeable field, we need to open transaction AIF/CUST • ERROR HANDLING • INTER-FACE SPECIFIC FEATURES and select the DEFINE CHANGE-ABLE FIELDS node in Figure 4.47. Next, you need to insert a new entry and in the field path field, define the field that should be enabled for editing in case of an error.

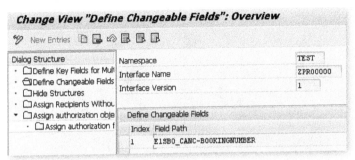

Figure 4.47: Defining changeable fields

From now on when AIF processes messages that end up with an error, it will be possible to edit it by double clicking on it as shown in Figure 4.48.

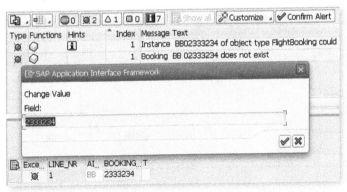

Figure 4.48: Editing the field in the Error and Monitoring transaction

All changes to the content of the fields are logged and can also be checked with transaction /AIF/ERROR_CHANGE_REPORT as shown in Figure 4.49. This report shows, among other things, the user who changed the content of the field along with old and new value of the field.

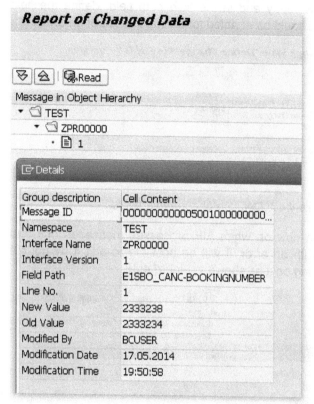

Figure 4.49: Report of changed data for field content changes

4.10 Snapshots

For monitoring purposes, sometimes it's necessary to check and compare statistics data for all interfaces to investigate the total number of messages, number of messages which were not processed correctly, or the cumulated number of log messages per each error type. AIF provides the option to take snapshots which can provide this information and you can generate it anytime. Creation of a new snapshot can be done by using the transaction /AIF/GENERATE_MSG_STAT_SNAP (Figure 4.50) where you need to specify the DATE that the snapshot should be generated for and the PACKAGE SIZE, which is the size of packages in which single messages are processed (the default size 1000 is suitable in most cases).

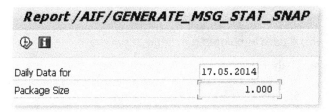

Figure 4.50: Snapshot generation

In the display snapshot transaction /AIF/DISPLAY_MSG_SNAPSHOTS you can select snapshots with snapshot ID, creation date, creation user, and the date the snapshot was created. Once you select the appropriate snapshot, you have several views you can use.

▶ Cumm. Msg. Statistics—this view can be used to list all statistics for messages available in the system at the time the snapshot was created.

▶ Daily Message Statistics—this view can be used to list all statistics for messages available in the system at the time of effective date specified in the snapshot.

▶ Cumm. Msg. Summary (see Figure 4.51)—this view can be used to list all log message available in the system at the time of the creation of the snapshot.

119

Cumulated Message Summary

Interface	Versi	M	Message Class	MsgCounter	Dt. Msg.Cn	Message text
ZPR00000	1	E	/AIF/MES	3	3	&1 &2 &3 &4
ZPR00000	1	E	BAPI	18	18	Instance &2&3 of object type &1 could not be
ZPR00000	1	E	BC_IBF	18	18	Booking &1 does not exist
ZPR00000	1	I	/AIF/ALERT	10	10	Alert already exists with ID &1 (category &2)
ZPR00000	1	I	/AIF/ALERT	6	3	Recipient list not found for interface &1/&2/&3
ZPR00000	1	I	/AIF/ALERT	20	15	Recipient contact not found for &1/&2/&3 and
ZPR00000	1	I	/AIF/MES	3	3	&1 &2 &3 &4
ZPR00000	1	I	/AIF/MES	54	18	Processing was completed
ZPR00000	1	I	/AIF/MES	18	18	Mapping has started
ZPR00000	1	W	/AIF/MES	18	18	Function &1 was not executed successfully
ZPR00000	1	E	/AIF/MES	3	3	&1 &2 &3 &4
ZPR00000	1	E	BAPI	18	18	Instance &2&3 of object type &1 could not be
ZPR00000	1	E	BC_IBF	18	18	Booking &1 does not exist
ZPR00000	1	I	/AIF/ALERT	10	10	Alert already exists with ID &1 (category &2)
ZPR00000	1	I	/AIF/ALERT	6	3	Recipient list not found for interface &1/&2/&3
ZPR00000	1	I	/AIF/ALERT	20	15	Recipient contact not found for &1/&2/&3 and

Figure 4.51: Cumulated message summary

▶ Daily Message Summary—this view can be used to list all log message available in the system for the effective data of the snapshot only.

5 Summary

SOA integration scenarios are more and more common in large SAP system environments. Different applications are being connected to each other in order to make the business more flexible and to allow it to adopt to new changing processes more quickly. SOA integration scenario monitoring is becoming an important part of daily activities and though there are many tools which support that activity and each of them has its own benefits, the most important thing is to get to know all features of the tools you might be using. Even the simplest Local Integration Engine monitor can be turned into a well performing monitoring platform if all of its features are being customized and set up. If this is not enough, we can always try more advanced monitoring applications like FEH/ECH or even the best of the breed among SAP monitoring application—AIF.

Most of the examples from this book were described as step-by-step configuration examples and hopefully any reader using any of those tools would be able to replicate the cases shown in the book without any problems. If this is the case, then the book served its purpose and the author did his job well.

espresso tutorials

You have finished the book.

A   The Author

Michał Krawczyk is a freelance SAP integration consultant with int4. He has been an SAP Mentor since 2007
and has been recognized for his SAP leadership includ-
ed winning the top contributor/topic leader award from
SDN (SAP Developer Network portal) in SAP PO/PI
eight times. Michał is the author of "Mastering idoc business scenarios with SAP XI", "Mastering idoc business
scenarios with SAP PI" (second edition) and "The Essen-
tials on SAP NetWeaver Process Integration" (A SAP
Mentor 2010 Series).

He is a regular contributor to the SAP Professional Jour-
nal, SAP CRM, SCM, Solution Manager, HR, SCM
online expert magazines. He is recognized as one of the
leading SAP integration experts in the world and has
written more than 140 articles and blogs on SDN
(*sdn.sap.com*), in addition to regularly speaking at SAP
events (SAP Techeds) on SAP PO/PI and SAP AIF.

Michał has consulted with clients in the food/beverage, consumer products, high tech and commodities industries on implementing SAP integration with SAP PI/PO, IDOC, ALE, CRM middleware technologies. He holds four SAP certifications including Development Consultant SAP—Exchange Infrastructure 3.0 Developer, SAP Certified Application Associate CRM Foundation with mySAP CRM 2005, mySAP SRM—Procurement Certified, and Development Consultant SAP NetWeaver—ABAP Workbench 2003.

B Index

C Disclaimer

Names used in this book, trade names, commodity names etc. can be brands even though they have no marking and as such are subject to legal requirements. All screenshots printed in this book are subject to copyright of SAP AG, Dietmar-Hopp-Allee 16, 69190 Walldorf, Germany.

This publication makes reference to products of SAP AG. SAP, R/3, SAP NetWeaver, Duet, PartnerEdge, ByDesign, SAP BusinessObjects Explorer, StreamWork, and other SAP products and services mentioned in the text, as well as the respective logos, are trademarks or registered trademarks of SAP AG in Germany and in other countries worldwide. Business Objects and the BusinessObjects logo, BusinessObjects, Crystal Reports, Crystal Decisions, Web Intelligence, Xcelsius, and other Business Objects products and services mentioned in the text as well as the respective logos are trademarks or registered trademarks of Business Objects Software Ltd. Business Objects is a company in the SAP AG group. Sybase and Adaptive Server, iAnywhere, Sybase 365, SQL Anywhere, and other Sybase products and services mentioned in the text as well as the respective logos are trademarks or registered trademarks of Sybase Inc. Sybase is a company in the SAP AG group. All other names of products and services are trademarks of the respective companies. The details in the text are not binding and are for information purposes only. Products may differ from country to country.

SAP Group shall not be liable for errors or omissions in this publication. The only warranties for SAP Group products and services are those that are set forth in the express warranty statements accompanying such products and services, if any. No further liability arises from the information contained in this publication.

More Espresso Tutorials eBooks

Ulrich Schlüter & Jörg Siebert:

SAP® HANA for ERP Financials

▶ Understanding the basics of SAP HANA

▶ Identify the potential of this technology

▶ Examine already existing HANA applications in SAP Financials

http://5019.espresso-tutorials.com/

Boris Rubarth:

First Steps in ABAP®

▶ Step-by-Step instructions for beginners

▶ Comprehensive descriptions and code examples

▶ A guide to create your first ABAP application

▶ Tutorials that provide answers to the most commonly asked programming questions

http://5015.espresso-tutorials.com/

Tanya Duncan:

The Essential SAP® Career Guide

▶ How to find a job with SAP

▶ Creating a stand-out SAP resume

▶ Choosing the right SAP module and how to develop skills in other modules

http://5012.espresso-tutorials.com/

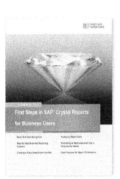

Anurag Barua:

First Steps in SAP® Crystal Reports

▶ Basic end-user navigation

▶ Creating a basic report from scratch

▶ Formatting to meet individual presentation needs

http://5017.espresso-tutorials.com/

Ingo Brenckmann & Mathias Pöhling:

The SAP® HANA Project Guide

▶ Delivering innovation with SAP HANA

▶ Creating a business case for SAP HANA

▶ Thinking in-memory

▶ Managing SAP HANA projects

http://5009.espresso-tutorials.com/

Coleen Bedrosian:

Six Sigma Implementation Guide

▶ Six Sigma and Lean Six Sigma concepts

▶ Available tools and how to use them

▶ The impact on an SAP implementation

http://5024.espresso-tutorials.com/

Darren Hague:

Universal Worklist with SAP NetWeaver® Portal

▶ Learn to easily execute business tasks using Universal Worklist

▶ Find in-depth advice on how to mak SAP workflows and alerts available

▶ Learn how to Include 3rd party workflows in SAP NetWeaver Portal

http://5076.espresso-tutorials.com